THRIVE

Also by Mark Hall

Lifestories
(with Tim Luke)

Your Own Jesus
(with Tim Luke)

The Well
(with Tim Luke)

THRIVE

DIGGING DEEP, REACHING OUT

MARK HALL
WITH TIM LUKE

ZONDERVAN

Thrive
Copyright © 2014 by Mark Hall

This title is also available as a Zondervan ebook.
Visit www.zondervan.com/ebooks.

Requests for information should be addressed to:

Zondervan, *Grand Rapids, Michigan* 49530

Library of Congress Cataloging-in-Publication Data

Hall, Mark, 1969-
    Thrive : digging deep and reaching out / Mark Hall, with Tim Luke. — 1st
[edition].
       pages cm
      ISBN 978-0-310-29334-7 (softcover)
      1. Christian life. I. Title.
    BV4501.3.H34825 2014
    248.4 — dc23   2013041231

Cover design: Tim Parker/Provident Label Group
Cover photography: iStockphoto LP
Interior photography: iStockphoto LP
Interior design: David Conn

Printed in the United States of America

14 15 16 17 18 19 20 21 22 /DCI/ 20 19 18 17 16 15 14 13 12 11 10 9 8 7 6 5 4 3 2

For Reagan Farris—
you've been my Timothy since you were young,
and I've watched you grow into one of my Pauls.
Your passion for Jesus, for his church,
and for your family challenges me.
We learned to thrive together.

Your brother,

Mark

CONTENTS

PART 2: REACHING OUT

CHAPTER 1

IF I CAN JUST . . .

You were meant to do more than just survive. You were meant to thrive.

You were not meant to struggle to make it through the week, the day, the next hour. You were not meant for your world to feel like a weight, for the break of dawn to be the starter pistol for another meaningless rat race. You were not meant to be shackled by anxiety, worry, and fear. No, you were meant for so much more.

You were meant to have life and to have it more abundantly. That is the promise of the eternal God.

You were meant to dig deep and to reach out.

You were meant to know God and to make him known.

You were meant to point to the one hope, the one anchor, the one true source of joy, peace, and contentment for the entire human race. His name is Jesus.

Surviving is for those who have no hope. That's not you — not if you're God's child.

You were meant to *thrive.*

I'm not saying you won't have trouble in this life. Only the false teachers of the prosperity gospel claim otherwise. They promise prosperity while using Scriptures written from prison or during some of the lowest moments in the lives of godly men. Out of Jesus' twelve disciples, only one escaped martyrdom, and he was exiled to a desolate island. I still can't figure how that entitles us to buy a Benz. Without exception, all of us will have some bad days. But Jesus tells us to take heart. He has overcome the world, which means we can thrive amid it all (John 16:33).

When I was in high school, the word *thrive* was not in my vocabulary. It felt like the best I could do was to survive. As I struggled with attention deficit disorder and dyslexia long before most folks knew of their existence, school days felt like a mix of labor camp, summer camp (recess and lunch), and the next embarrassment that lurked right around the corner. At times, my life still feels that way. At times, I feel like I'm still trying to survive.

If we are honest, we can look back on the last year and say we only survived it. We survived work. We survived school. We survived with most of our relationships intact.

Some of us have not survived very well. Maybe our circle

of friends has changed. Maybe our families are different than they were this time last year, and we have survived some major storms. In fact, a lot of us are in survival mode right now:

If I can just get to this weekend . . .

If I can just make it to the first of the month . . .

If I can just get to summer vacation . . .

If I can just finish this project . . .

If I can just beat this sickness . . .

If I can just make this payment . . .

If I can just get the kids through college . . .

I remember looking at the clock in high school and thinking, *Only eleven more minutes. I don't think they're ever going to pass. I'm never going to get out of this place. I'm going to grow old and die in this room. If I can survive just eleven more minutes, I'm done with this.*

If you're not careful, you will live your life with that same survival attitude.

I went to my class reunion a few years ago. As I talked with a group of friends, we looked over to the bar. Around it stood ten guys who are the exact same people they were as seniors in high school. They never grew up. My wife, Melanie, and I sat with a friend named Karen. Back when we were in school, Karen was quiet — nice, but reserved. Believe it or not, I was too. Neither of us really did much in high school, which is sad when I think about it. It wasn't until later in life that we emerged from our shells. At the reunion, Karen looked at the guys at the bar and shook her head.

"You know," she said, "it seems like some people never left the beach."

We listened to the guys at the bar say things like "Man, I was glad to just punch that clock Friday" and "Dude, I can't wait till summer. We're heading down to Panama City Beach."

Surviving.

Every day, they're just surviving.

You were not made to survive life. Or to survive work. Or school. Or your family. You were not made to exist until you can get over the next hump or get to the next break. You were created for one purpose: *to know God and to make him known*.

You are not living the life you were created to live if *survive* is your word. You were made to *thrive*.

Point to Remember

We were meant to thrive and not just survive.

CHAPTER 2

BALANCED
IS BOTH

A certain tree has become a source of inspiration to me. Somehow the tree keeps popping up in everything I do. I've spoken about it in concerts and to student groups. I even used it as an illustration in one of my previous books, *Your Own Jesus*.

Now my student ministry is called Thrive. This book is called *Thrive*. Casting Crowns' latest album is called *Thrive*. And that album includes a song called "Thrive."

The tree is located at a spot in Geneva, Alabama, named The Junction because it sits at the confluence of the Choctawhatchee River and the Pea River. I was on staff at nearby First Baptist Church of Samson early in my career as a youth pastor. For most of the last decade, I have served as co-student pastor with Reagan Farris at Eagle's Landing First Baptist Church in McDonough, Georgia. Reagan was one of the students in my youth group at Samson. Several years ago, Reagan and I took our Eagle's Landing student group back home to Samson on a ministry tour. I wanted everyone to see The Tree.

When we were growing up in South Alabama, we always called it The Tree. You know it must be special when a tree gets a name—and that name is just The Tree. In that region, if you ever said, "Hey, we're going to The Tree," everybody knew what you meant. The mammoth oak tree is more than three hundred years old. It's been around longer than the United States of America.

The Tree sits on the banks of The Junction, so the rivers have always watered it. We asked some of our students to stretch out their arms, join hands, and make a circle around The Tree. It took eight or nine guys to do it. In California, this wouldn't be a big deal; the redwoods out there are gargantuan. But in Alabama, The Tree is a tourist attraction. We had our tall pine trees and the occasional thick oak, but it's odd to see a tree of this enormity. Its main limbs are bigger than most trees in my neighborhood. One person can't reach all the way around many of its limbs and some of them are so heavy they bend almost to the ground.

We had sixty students on the trip, and all of us climbed into The Tree at one time to sit or stand on the branches for a photo. No one was standing on the ground.

About every ten years, the two rivers flood the area. So there are mud lines on that tree. There's a bike up in that tree. The water has risen many times and taken just about everything away—everything except that tree.

I believe we can find a lesson in there somewhere.

An old farmer in overalls joined us at The Tree. He talked like a Southern version of Morgan Freeman. His voice alone made me believe everything he said.

"You know, the reason these kinds of trees are so strong is, not only are they planted by the water, but they have just as much going on under the ground as they do above the ground," he said. "If you wiped all of the dirt out of here, you'd basically see this." He held up one hand on top of the other, palms facing us and fingers spread wide. He wanted us to see how the tree's roots had spread underground just as wide as the branches had spread above ground.

A little later, Psalm 1 came to my mind, and I read it to our group.

> Blessed is the man
>> who walks not in the counsel of the wicked,
> nor stands in the way of sinners,
>> nor sits in the seat of scoffers;
> but his delight is in the law of the LORD,
>> and on his law he meditates day and night.
> He is like a tree
>> planted by streams of water
> that yields its fruit in its season,
>> and its leaf does not wither.
> In all that he does, he prospers.

Psalm 1:1–3

I call these the Thrive Verses. They portray what happens when we dig our roots deep.

I didn't realize it at the time, but my life's ministry originated out of this simple idea for a devotional moment alongside a giant tree. It dawned on me that, like the big oak tree, growth as a believer requires two parts. We have to *dig our roots deep*. And when we do, we naturally will *reach out*.

When we grow roots, we dive into God's Word and prayer and learn from other believers. As we reach out, we show Jesus to people and tell them about him. A balanced believer is supposed to do both. Still, it's easy to pick one side or the other and get comfortable, resigning ourselves to the thought that some people are "roots" people and some are "reach" people.

I'm more of a roots person by nature. The personalities and interests of roots people bend toward the serious side. We understand the importance of Bible study and theology, and we like to go deep. Too often, however, we keep it all tucked under the surface. When we get around people, it's like they're in our way until we can get to the next Bible study. We have great discipline, but sometimes we're useless to everyone around us.

At too many other times, I've seen people who concentrate solely on reaching out. They want to serve everybody and feed everybody and hang out with everybody and change everybody. But a lot of times, their roots are shallow. They're never in the Word for themselves, and they're all about *doing* rather than *being*. They're out trying to save the world, and when the first storm blows in, what happens? They're like tumbleweeds that topple over and roll along because they have no roots.

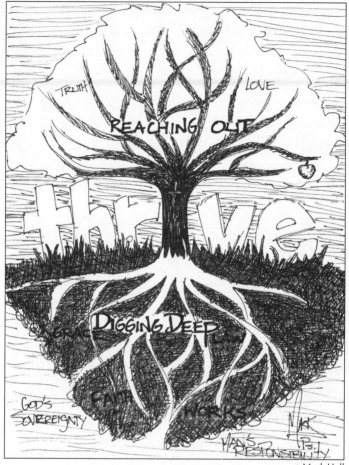

© Mark Hall

It's a simple concept. To thrive, we must:

- *Dig deep* into the roots of our relationship with Jesus. This helps us understand who God is and who we are in him. We dig in to know God.
- *Reach out* to others. This helps us to show the world that we belong to Jesus and that Jesus is God. We reach out to make God known.

Inspired by the giant oak tree in Alabama, I sketched a logo for our student ministry at Eagle's Landing (see illlustration on previous page). It depicts a healthy believer who has both roots and reach.

The empty promises of the world define success and contentment in terms of money, possessions, prestige, and power. The Bible's definition of the word *thrive* means digging deep into a personal relationship with Jesus and reaching out to others with his truth and love—to know God and to make him known.

I wrote this book in two sections—Digging Deep and Reaching Out. Together we will explore God's sovereignty, human responsibility, truth, and love. I know that can sound like a lot of heavy teaching, but I really don't think you'll find it overwhelming at all. Above all, I hope you will end up encouraged and inspired to thrive with the abundant and balanced life that Christ promises is available for all of us.

May these words from my song "Thrive" be the marching cadence for us all:

Into your Word we're digging deep
To know the Father's heart.
Into the world we're reaching out
To show them who you are.

Point to Remember
Balanced believers dig their roots deep
and reach out to others.

PART 1

DIGGING DEEP

CHAPTER 3

UNKNOWNS

God has a dream for you.

His dream doesn't necessarily include prosperity or good health or even what most people would describe as happiness. He's not interested in making you comfortable. His dreams for you are much bigger than any of those pursuits. You were made to thrive in more than a worldly kind of way. You were made to thrive in Jesus. God's dream for you is to know him and make him known, to dig deep into his Word and to plumb his depths and to reach out — to live in such a way that you point to the one true hope for all people.

It seems to be a spiritual contradiction, but it's not. When you finally do let go, you finally grasp what God wants and has for you. Surrendering to Jesus is the way not only to abundant life, but also to life itself. I grew up in church before I learned this the hard way.

I was nineteen when a long-term relationship with a girl crashed and burned. I didn't know what to do. I described in my book *Your Own Jesus* how I held a gun in my hands and considered taking my life. My saving hope was that there was more to Jesus than the church I'd grown up in, and that's when I started to see growth.

I waded into God's Word, and in a three-month period, my life changed forever. I discovered my own walk with Jesus. I discovered that God wanted me to do something in his church, which baffled me because to that point I didn't really know what people in the church did ("They really work only one day a week!"). I also began to see Melanie, who had been one of my best friends for years, as something other than my friend. She had always been attractive to me, but I figured we'd always just be friends. Out of nowhere, we started dating at about the same time I began singing songs in the car. Never in my life had I even considered the notion of writing a song. I started making up little prayers to melodies that popped in my head.

I got all excited to do something for God. That's when I laid my plans.

First, I married Melanie. We dated for about four months. When you've been friends for eleven years, there's really not much else to get to know.

We moved to Graceville, Florida, so I could go to Bible college. I knew I could pursue music because I sang with my dad in church. I was convinced God had planned this path for me. Not until I arrived at college did reality hit.

I was like Peter stepping into the waves or David facing Goliath. Those are two of the biggest visuals in my early walk with God—the idea of storms, waves, giants, trouble, and doubt. Those recurring themes appear somewhere in most of my records because of the events in this window of time.

I walked onto campus and straight into the music version of "Welcome to the NFL." It literally was the first time it occurred to me that I was attempting to go to *college*. Suddenly I realized I'd have to take courses other than music to get a degree. And for the music classes, it would have helped if I'd known how to read music—but I didn't.

I quickly learned that gravity is real and waves don't hold weight. I almost tanked college in that first week. There I was, facing this calling from God and trying to figure out how to go about it when my perspective changed. Suddenly the God part was blurry and the obstacles were crystal clear. I was frozen in fear and doubt.

That's when I got into 2 Corinthians 12 and learned from Paul that God uses our weaknesses. Where we're weak, he's strong.

I remember hearing about Ken Medema, a piano guy who wrote a song called "Moses." It's a powerful story song that you can find on YouTube. He describes Moses in the wilderness, which is where I felt I was in Graceville. Maybe the song is not your style, but it was a big deal to me, even when I didn't have any depth to my walk with Jesus.

That song echoed the truth that God uses the weak things in the world to shame the wise, and it was where my *but* almost got in the way. Christians have huge *buts*, where we believe everything *but* [insert excuse here]. If you believe something *but*, there's a good chance you don't believe it at all. There's a chance you just know it and it's on your T-shirt, but it's not the filter through which you run your actions.

On my first day of college, I knew all of my little life-lesson moments and memory verses from high school, like "I can do all things through Christ who strengthens me." But then I failed—with a big, fat zero—the entrance exam for music majors.

The music department's response was to ask me to come in and sing. When I did, they were like, "Oh. OK." I guess somewhere between my audition and their feeling sorry for me, they decided to start me in remedial core courses to see if I could survive. I think it was a low enrollment year for them.

Along with my cruddy ACT scores that few schools would have accepted, nothing logical told me I should be enrolled in college. All of the superstars from the huge churches were there and sounded awesome. I fought through the insecurity of it all and sat at a piano to write a song called "Fear." It was a sparse little ballad that lacked a chorus. Years later, Steven Curtis Chapman wrote a chorus and handed it back to me. You may know that song. It's called "Voice of Truth." It came from the idea, borne out repeatedly in Scripture, that God uses unknowns to make him known.

I thought of David and how he defeated Goliath. I

thought of the little boy with the five loaves and two fish and how Jesus used his lunch to feed thousands. I realized that this indigent little boy had to have some faith. I'd never thought about it, but he willingly gave up his lunch for others. Somewhere in there, I had to decide whether I believed all this Bible stuff was real.

The more I looked at Scripture, the more I found broken people rather than whole people—people like Moses, David, Peter, and Mary. I saw how the weak overcome the strong. The poor have an easier time getting into heaven than the rich. Everything the world calls success I didn't find in the Word, and I learned that God takes you just as you are.

In the middle of all this, I still went to class, made bad grades, and landed on academic probation. I also discovered my idea of a music career wasn't everything that God had for me. The music was just a means to another means. God wanted me to be a youth pastor.

I went to First Baptist of Samson and started telling some of these stories to my kids. That's all I knew to do. I could tell good stories. But I'd never told anyone I was dyslexic. I never talked about it because I didn't realize I had dyslexia until Bruce White, my college English professor, told me I had it.

"No, I don't," I said. I wasn't even sure what dyslexia meant.

"Yeah, I think you do," he said. "Look how you're writing your notes here. When you fill out a form, do you write one of your names in this blank and then look over and write your zip code and then go down to the other side of the page and write your phone number and then come back up to your last name and then write your address?"

I swallowed. *He's reading my mail to me right now*, I thought. *Melanie always yells at me because I can't fill out forms.*

One by one, he started naming symptoms, and I had every one of them. Then we took an ADD test in psychology, and it was the only test on which I scored 100 in college. I was in learning disabled classes as a kid, which was embarrassing, but I'd never put together the reasons for my struggles with academics and learning. College is a heck of a place to learn you have dyslexia.

Whichever way I read it — mixed-up words and all — the idea that God has bigger dreams for me than I do sprang to life.

Point to Remember:

God's dreams for us are bigger than our own.

CHAPTER 4

A BETTER DREAM

Throughout Scripture, God approaches different people with the same message: "I know you have plans and you have this idea about how you're going to pull off life. But I have something else for you."

God told each of them that he knew how to make them thrive.

First Samuel 16 contains the beginning of the story of David, a teenager who had his own ideas of how his life would unfold. I'm sure he dreamed of bigger and better things than just tending his father's livestock. He didn't long to sit in a pasture his whole life and count sheep: "One, two, three, four—yep, they're all here."

Can you imagine the downtime as he sat on a hill and

watched his sheep feed? Any time a guy has downtime, he dreams. He's thinking, *One day, I'm going to be in a better place and have a better career and people are going to respect me.* David learned how to hunt. He learned how to use a sling. He learned how to play a harp and sing.

Like all of us, David had dreams. Maybe one shepherd down the road was the talk of the town because he had three times more sheep, and David always had to hear about the guy and his awesome farm. He had to hear the stories of his older brothers' exploits. He got tired of the "Isn't he cute?" pat on the head, even when he was trying to say something serious.

David had to think, *One day I'll own the sheep on a thousand hills. People will all come to me and ask, "How did you do it? How did you take thirty sheep and turn them into this massive flock?"*

We're always crafting our acceptance speeches before we've ever done a thing. I talk to teenagers every day who are starting a band and want to know how they can make it to the next level. When I ask questions, I usually hear, "Well, we actually haven't had a rehearsal yet."

"OK. Do you have any songs?"

"Uh, we've written a few lines."

"Uh-huh. Have you guys even met? Do you know the members of the band yet?" They're planning their Grammy speech before they've tuned a guitar.

As I thought about David, a question popped into my mind. *What do our dreams sound like to God?*

I imagined God listening to David's thoughts and dreams, knowing that David loved him and had a heart for him. The more I learned David's story, I could just hear God whispering to him in a breezy pasture: "I know you have dreams and plans, which is awesome. But my dream for you will not even fit in your head. In fact, I can't even tell you everything yet."

The Bible reveals that God shares tiny snippets with David as they walk together. "Here's what we're going to do. There's a valley with a ten-foot giant down there, and I have a special job for you. I'm going to get your dad to send you down there to get lunch, because you'd freak out if I told you my plans. But don't worry. I've been setting up this moment your whole life."

Josh Mix is one of our guitar players in Casting Crowns. He was twenty-two years old when he joined the band. He never auditioned once. He just served in our church, used his talents, played his songs, and worked with a bunch of teenagers, some who can play and some who can't carry a note. He did all the grunt work that goes with it, plugging in cords and amps and foot pedals and conducting sound checks and rehearsals and practices. He had no idea I was watching everything he did.

He walked in one day, and I said, "Hey, Hector Cervantes is leaving the band. I want you to be the new guitar player."

His mouth fell open. "Are you serious?" he said. "Let me pray about it . . . Um, amen. Yeah, I'm in. What do you want me to do?"

That's how God arranges our lives. He lets us chase our

little sparks of inspiration until he's ready to move us in his perfect timing. All along, he orchestrates our lives to where he can speak through his Word, his Holy Spirit, and our circumstances to confirm what he wants.

When David faced Goliath, he didn't have a landmark conversation to recall so he could say, "God told me I was going to win." Rather, God had orchestrated David's circumstances to give him confidence in his present challenge. He had emboldened David through encounters with a lion and a bear, and David was able to recount those victories when facing Goliath.

"I brought you through those moments," God said, "and I'll bring you through this."

So what does David say to prepare for Goliath? "God brought me through that. He'll bring me through this."

God does the same with us.

As I thought about God maneuvering David's life and giving David his dream for him, I imagined God saying, "Here's what I'm thinking. Let's go down here and take care of this little problem with the giant and get the army back on track. Um, it's going to be a little rough with the king for a while, maybe a spear thrown at your head. You may have to go on the lam and bounce from cave to cave for a bit. But I'll be there with you."

Even with all of the challenges and hardships in God's dream for David, David's own dreams could not compare.

David's dreams were probably in a box. I'm pretty sure he

never thought, *I'm going to behead a ten-foot giant in front of the entire army and then become king of Israel to establish a royal line through which the Savior of the human race will come.*

David's dreams probably included a big livestock operation or maybe a career writing songs and leading worship at synagogue. God looked at David and saw something else. He saw the genealogy of Jesus.

Mary, the mother of Jesus, had dreams too. Can you see her scurrying to clean the house and help her mom cook supper while she thought about her fellow? She was engaged to be married to Joseph and had dreams of keeping her own home and livestock. Perhaps she imagined a woodworking business for Joseph.

"Everybody talks about Joseph. We're going to have kids and grow old together. Maybe we'll even have a son, which would be awesome because Joseph is the best carpenter around. People come from miles around to ask him to build stuff for them and to see his work. He has a piece of furniture in every house in this town, and the idea of teaching his boy how to do this and passing on his business is amazing. It could be Joseph and Son Builders, Inc."

God sat back and listened to her little heart dream away.

"That's a great dream, Mary. But just like David, who's a little bit connected to this picture too, your dream is in a box. You have one box where you keep what you think you can do. You have another box where you keep what you think

I can do. I have a better dream for you. We're on the same page about Joseph. I think he's a fine fellow. But I've been watching your life and preparing you for what I'm about to do in you, and you didn't even know it. If I had told you when you were a kid that you were going to be the mother of one called Jesus, we wouldn't be able to fit your head in your house. You wouldn't have been able to handle any of this.

"Here's my dream for you: I'm going to save the world like I promised in the stories you've heard from your dad and his dad and his dad. It's time. The Messiah is coming. I want the perfect mom to raise him. And I want that mom to be you."

That conversation, in words to the same effect, happened through the angel Gabriel.

God didn't explain away all the details. He didn't curb the difficulties. He didn't even say, "It'll be a little awkward with Joseph for a while. You'll hit some rough patches. And childbirth is still going to hurt." But he dreamed much bigger for her than she ever dreamed.

God is not finished working in his world. God is not finished with you.

How we face the future and how we make decisions are based on what we believe about God and what we believe about ourselves. We can say God is in control, but our lives often suggest that we don't totally buy it. We can say that God forgives sin and wipes it away forever, but we still live under guilt.

God wants to use the Romans 12:1–2 Effect on us. He wants to renew our minds and redefine our ideas of who he is and who we are in him. We believe about him only what we've seen. We have fuzzy notions of him and partially believe what we've read, heard, and sung about him. But we'd be amazed to realize how much of our faith is still not ours.

I discovered this in how we pray for people. When somebody else is dangerously sick, we pray for "God's will," not for healing, because we're afraid the person won't pull through and we don't want to stick out our necks in public. But if it's my kid, I'm not praying for "God's will." That's my boy, and I'm begging God to heal him! Our just-in-case prayers tell us something about our view of God.

David, who is called a man after God's own heart, asks God to search him and know his heart (Psalm 139:23). He basically says, "I don't even know my own heart. I don't know why I do the things I do, and I don't understand my motives."

I have to dig deep into my roots so God can show me who he is and who I am in him. He has to redefine what saved me and keeps me saved. He has to redefine real fruit. I let him redefine wrong ideas about him and about me. I let him search me and know my heart. I let him have his way.

Despite my shortcomings, God has been patient and kind, long-suffering and forgiving. Even when I take the wrong turn, he turns it around for my good. Love from other people doesn't work that way. Jobs don't work that way. Spouses don't even work that way.

I've let the world tell me what forgiveness means. I've let the job market define my skill set. I've let the SAT or ACT define for me how smart I am. This label that people hung around me when I was sent to learning disabled classes convinced me that I didn't need to get on stage in front of anybody. God had to work on me awhile to get a lot of gunk out of my head, and it's still in there whispering even as I sing in front of thousands of people.

So I got in his Word and I got on my knees and I got to know God. I learned how to put all my weight on him. I dug my roots deep into his Word and obeyed his nudges to reach out to others. I let the Lord work out of me what he had worked into me. I learned how to share his love with the truth. I committed my life to know him and make him known.

All the while, God bided his time and worked out his dream for me. All the while, he taught me to thrive.

Point to Remember

God orchestrates his dreams for us despite our lesser goals and our mistakes.

CHAPTER 5

THE EAGLE AND
THE YARDBIRD

Nestled in a valley between two mammoth mountains stood a small farm. It had a few crops and some pigs and cows, and farthest to the rear, tucked at the edge of the woods, was a large fenced chicken coop.

At the top of the highest mountain, a solitary tree branch extended over a jagged cliff. In that branch sat an eagle's nest. Mama Eagle warmed her eggs as she surveyed her vast kingdom and decided it was time to find a bite to eat. She knew she couldn't be gone long. She could sense the life inside the eggs starting to stir.

After she flew away, a storm blew through the mountain range. A wind gust lifted one side of the nest so that the egg closest to the rim rolled out of the nest. The egg plummeted toward the valley below but happened to land in the middle of a soft fir tree branch. It dropped to another limb below, then another, then landed in a bank of gentle clover, and somehow—by reasons only a youth pastor's story can explain—rolled all the way down the valley, underneath the fence of the chicken coop, up the henhouse ramp, and straight into the nest of the largest hen on the farm.

Mama Hen strolled up and saw all the eggs. It dawned on her that she had failed math in school. She had one more egg than she remembered, and it was the biggest of the bunch. She settled in for the night, a little befuddled but content with her larger nest of eggs.

A few days later, the eggs hatched. One chick. Two chicks. Three chicks. The larger egg on the left side started to tremble, then shake. The next thing Mama Hen knew, a beak popped out that didn't look like any of the others.

As the rest of the shell fell away, the ugliest chicken in the coop wobbled to life. Mama Hen's beak fell open as she shook her head. "Well, he's mine. I'm just gonna love him, bless his heart." She named him Iggy.

The farmer called his chickens "yardbirds," but Mama Hen kept her ugly son hidden when the farmer came talking to his yardbirds and throwing feed.

Iggy grew up with all the chickens. He learned to eat like a chicken and walk like a chicken. On the first day of Yardbird School, the teacher lined up all of her students and taught them how to peck corn feed from the ground. Iggy couldn't get it right. Nothing the yardbirds did seemed natural. While the rest of the chicks learned to deftly nip one end of a small earthworm, their big brother snapped a large lizard in two with his sharp beak.

One evening just before bedtime, lightning flashed and thunder roared. It shook the coop so hard that the little birdies screamed and ran under their mother's wing. Not Iggy. The little eaglet streaked to the top of the coop, expanded his chest to twice its normal size, and shrieked into the dusk air.

Mama Hen was not happy. "You get back here, Iggy! Who do you think you are?"

"Um. I'm not sure. It just felt natural to holler back."

"Well, we don't holler back. And we surely don't shriek. Yardbirds cluck. From now on, you will cluck."

Another day, the neighbor's cat slowly crept up to the coop. Mama Hen and the teacher spotted the cat and started clucking and ushering the chicks back inside. But Iggy let out a high-pitched shrill, spread wide his fledgling wings, and jumped straight toward the cat and into the wire fence. The collision with the fence was so violent that the cat jumped a foot in the air and darted into the brush.

The other yardbirds walked up to Iggy. "What in the world are you doing? Where did you learn to do that?"

"I don't know," Iggy said. "I just felt like something needed to be done."

"Well, you can't do that. We're yardbirds. This is what

we do—we peck and we run and we cluck. That's it. Pretty much in that order. Understand?"

Iggy made sure he stayed in line thereafter, and soon he learned to blend in with the yardbirds as best he could. He still towered over his brothers and sisters with his white head, curved beak, long black feathers, and huge wingspan. But he followed the crowd so long that eventually he became one of them.

After years of learning their ways and falling in with the crowd, Iggy became the perfect yardbird.

Years later, Iggy and his siblings were as old and gray as yardbirds can get. One day, Iggy's youngest brother looked into the sky and said, "What's that?" All heads turned skyward. At first no one could make out the figure against the sun. Was it a plane? A chicken hawk?

Another yardbird finally broke the silence as a shrill whistle pierced the sky. "Oh, I know what that is. That, my friends, is the majestic eagle."

"Ooohh," said all the other yardbirds in unison.

The giant eagle soared over them, wings fluttering and pristine white head cocked to display his piercing, golden brown eyes. All the yardbirds gawked at him with equal parts admiration and fear.

"Can you imagine being something like that?" one sibling said. "We got to be yardbirds. But *that* thing got to be an eagle."

Another sibling shook its head and blinked its eyes. "I

sure wish I could be an eagle." He smiled and threw the elbow of his wing into Iggy's side.

"Me too," Iggy said. "Me too."

Iggy had the talons, the beak, the wings, the chest, the eyes, the strength, the senses, and the instincts to do everything an eagle needs to do. He was the total package. But in his head, he could never get past how he grew up and what everyone else told him. He let fear, doubt, and circumstances keep him from being who he was meant to be.

So much of how we see God and how we see ourselves is shaped by our experiences and by what others say to us and about us. Too little of what we believe about God and ourselves is shaped by what he tells us in his Word. We would do well to dig into the truth more often. How can we know what to believe in a particular trial or circumstance when we don't know his Word? The only way any of us will ever thrive is if we first learn Scripture and then just take him at his Word.

Believe him, friend. Dive deep into his Word. Beg him to speak to you as you earnestly seek him, pour out your heart to him, and pour into your roots. You draw your sustenance, your lifeblood, from your spiritual roots.

What are you feeding your roots?

We all were yardbirds once. Only God can transform a yardbird into an eagle. But when God has made you an eagle, only you can choose to live like a yardbird.

Along with certain gifts, God gives you his Holy Spirit and daily opportunities to bring him glory. That falls under his sovereignty. But sooner or later, you've got to spread your wings, overcome your fear, and soar. That falls under your responsibility. But notice what comes first — God's sovereignty. In the next chapter, I'll show you how one of my favorite verses in Ephesians explains God's role and our role.

Point to Remember

*God in his sovereignty has a plan for our lives,
but it's up to us to respond in obedience.*

CHAPTER 6

BUT GOD

God is sovereign. This means he is supreme and always in control. The Bible says no one comes to the Father unless the Holy Spirit draws him. In both physical and spiritual ways, God started you, sustains you, and will complete you.

God's existence and sovereignty are the most fundamental beliefs we can possess — the very core of our deepest roots. When we dig in to know God more, we are tapping into the infiniteness of his love, grace, mercy, forgiveness, power, and sovereignty. Nothing or no one is greater. He sees all, knows all, and controls all. Whatever happens in your life, God either brings it or allows it for his good reasons. Scripture tells us that ultimately he does everything for his glory and for our good (Romans 8:28). Spending time with him helps wrap our roots around these unchangeable truths.

When I walk through the book of Ephesians with someone, I like to spend a little extra time in chapter 2. "All right," I say, "I want you to read this and look for yourself in this section, and then I want you to read it again and look for God."

The first part of the passage focuses on who we were and where we were without God, and I stress those words as I read them aloud. The second part focuses on who God is and what he did for us, and I stress those words too.

First, here's the *you* in Ephesians 2:

And *you* were dead in the trespasses and sins in which *you* once walked, following the course of this world, following the prince of the power of the air, the spirit that is now at work in the *sons* of disobedience— among whom *we* all once lived in the passions of *our* flesh, carrying out the desires of the *body* and the *mind*, and were by nature *children* of wrath, like the rest of *mankind*.

Ephesians 2:1–3, emphasis added

Quite a list of accomplishments. We should be so proud.

Now read what God did:

But *God*, being rich in mercy, because of the great love with which *he* loved us, even when we were dead in our trespasses, made us alive together with *Christ*—by grace you have been saved—and raised us up with *him* and seated us with *him* in the heavenly places in *Christ Jesus*, so that in the coming ages *he* might show the immeasurable riches of *his* grace in kindness toward us in *Christ Jesus*. For by grace you have been saved through faith. And this is not your own doing; it is the gift of *God*, not a result of works, so that no one may boast.

Ephesians 2:4–9, emphasis added

Now, what was our part in this? We were dead. We sinned. We blew it over and over.

What was God's part? He did it all. He chose us, made us alive, lavished his grace on us, started us, and will complete what he started.

The next few verses go on to emphasize that at one time we were separated from Christ, without hope and without God. Now that God has saved us, we have been brought near to God by the blood of Christ, and he himself is our peace.

If you think you did something to start your relationship with God, it's only logical to think you could do something to end it. You can either rest in your picture of God or be haunted by it. This passage helps us determine whether we have painted a biblical picture of God and of ourselves. I can't think of a better reason to study Scripture. Especially the part about understanding God.

One of the added blessings of being in Casting Crowns is that we get to be involved with a ministry called Teen Challenge. The word *teen* is in their name, but they help people of all ages who struggle with addictions or life-controlling problems.

If a Teen Challenge center is in the vicinity of one of our concerts, we let their students serve on our crew for the day. I know I'm going to have several touches with them, so I try to get to know them throughout the day. I learn their names in the morning, ask them about something in their lives in the afternoon, and then hopefully get a chance to deal with something they're going through before we pack up and leave.

At one particular concert after a snowstorm up north, I met a guy I'll call Steve. He was about twenty-two years old, a tall man who wore a dark heavy-metal T-shirt and a denim vest. He had a long, curly beard, and hair down to his shoulders. As big and mean as he wanted to look, I could tell he was hurting. I knew he had a soft heart just from talking to him that morning. He didn't make much eye contact. Life had beaten him down.

Later, I invited him to come to the band's prayer time after sound check. My devotional that day was from Psalm 63:1–4:

> O God, you are my God; earnestly I seek you;
>> my soul thirsts for you;
> my flesh faints for you,
>> as in a dry and weary land where there is no water.
> So I have looked upon you in the sanctuary,
>> beholding your power and glory.
> Because your steadfast love is better than life,
>> my lips will praise you.
> So I will bless you as long as I live;
>> in your name I will lift up my hands.

I asked the group these questions: "Have you figured out yet that you live in a dry and weary land? Somewhere in the back of your mind, do you still think that something in this world is going to do it for you? A lot of people are searching for something to fulfill them. We all want to get to the verse that says we want to see God in the sanctuary, behold his power and glory, and experience a love that is better than life. We want to skip to that verse, but we can't because we haven't resigned ourselves to the truth in the first verse, which is that this world is a dry and weary land that cannot fill us."

Steve heard the devotional and hung around afterward. We didn't get into a deep spiritual conversation because he was a little standoffish. That night, he sat to the left of our sound board during the concert. I kept looking at him, because whenever I make a connection with one of the Teen Challenge guys—or anyone else I meet before our concerts—whatever I say on stage that night is for those people. I pick out a handful of folks to talk to because it helps me focus better.

Steve seemed glued to everything he heard. He was one of the crew guys, so he was loving the lights and the music, but I also sensed God working on his heart. After the show, I approached the crew and thanked all of the Teen Challenge and local helpers for their work. I walked up to Steve and tried to see if I could break through his barrier.

"What do you think about all of this—about everything you've heard?" I asked.

"Oh, I think it's real good," he said. "Real good."

I tried to stretch the conversation, but that's about as deep as it got. To my knowledge, Steve didn't surrender to Jesus as his Savior that night, but I could tell that God had begun to redefine himself to Steve. Before that day, he did not have the correct picture of God. In Steve's head, God picked others around him, because everything about his demeanor said what he thought of himself: *I'm a crew guy. I'm a class below these people. I'll never be in that group. I could never be one of the churchy people. I'll never be one of the people in front of everybody. This is just who I am and all I'll ever be.*

I asked Steve how I could pray for him. He had a relative who was sick. I prayed for the relative, and I asked God to continue to pursue Steve and stay in his thoughts and not let him take his mind off of anything he had heard that day.

Several months later, Steve showed up at one of our concerts. He drove four hours to get there and brought his dad. He had also made a great connection with our drummer, Brian Scoggin. The next night, we were another four hours away, and he came again and spent the day with Brian. God is still working on Steve, and I'm still praying for him.

We have to let God paint for us the picture of who he is. If we paint our own picture of God, he'll look a lot like our dads (for better or worse) and a lot like how love works down here on earth. And you know how it is — people will love us *as long as* and *until*. But there is always a line that human love won't cross. That's not what God's love is like.

You're going to attach your idea of God to what you know. If you don't know what he says about who he is, how are you going to get to know him? If you let God define himself for you and let him define you for you, now you're ready to start blooming. We operate on a faulty root system when we go by our own logic. We choose the finite over the infinite.

At the base of our roots must be the understanding that we did not figure this out; we did not turn over a new leaf; we did not decide one day that we were going to try this Jesus thing. The closest we can ever come with our own efforts is religion, and it will not grow. Religion has no roots.

First Corinthians 1:8 states that Jesus "will sustain you to the end, guiltless in the day of our Lord Jesus Christ." What God starts, he finishes.

The fun part comes in between.

Point to Remember

God is sovereign. We did nothing to begin the relationship. He did it all.

CHAPTER 7

REDEFINING REALITY

One weekend several years ago, the adult women workers in our student ministry took the girls on a retreat. With our wives out of town, a few of us guys grew bored in about twenty-three minutes. As most wives know, guys don't really plan things. We just do them. I wondered aloud what we should do, and somebody hit the default button. "Let's go see what's at the theater."

Reagan Farris and a few other guys piled into my car. Once we reached the theater, we paused on the sidewalk to check out the movie titles.

"Let's go see this one," one of the guys said, pointing to the poster of a movie called *The Grudge*.

"I don't know, man," I said. "I used to go see horror movies all the time as a kid, and I just don't need that stuff in my head."

"Oh, come on," he said. "It'll be good."

"I don't know. Nah, I don't think so."

"Oh, come on," he said. "Come on, come on, come on."

Then he started the whole bro thing. He looked at me and cracked a wry smile: "Dude . . ."

"Nah, man."

"Dude . . ."

I shook my head.

"Dude."

Sigh. "Fine. Let's go."

There I was, clergy, man of the cloth, elder, overseer — all of those terms — and I just got peer pressured into doing something I knew I shouldn't do. I have a personal conviction against horror movies. Everything they pump into my head and my heart screams "old life" instead of "new life in Christ." Still, *The Grudge* had a decent rating (PG-13). So I relented. I'm pretty picky about the movies I watch. I'm not going to pay ten bucks to see sexual stuff or hear God's name taken in vain. But this movie wasn't like that.

It was just . . .

It was life scarring.

In the first thirty seconds, I knew I would never be the

same. The opening credits had barely rolled when I felt that creepy feeling from childhood that reaches down, grabs your gut, and rattles you to the core. Scene after scene, I kept thinking, *That's going to stay with me. That's going to come back to haunt me later.*

It grew worse. Horror movies and salty popcorn don't mix. Horror movies produce adrenaline. Adrenaline makes your heart pound. So does sodium. A pounding heart races blood through your kidneys. And your kidneys fill your bladder. The $40 Guzzler drink probably didn't help either.

Halfway through, I couldn't take it anymore. "I've got to go to the bathroom," I said.

We were at a giant cineplex with dozens of theaters. The closest bathroom seemed to stretch half the building away, which now reminded me of the hotel hallways in *The Shining*. See, another horror movie from my childhood. They never leave.

The bathroom had stall after stall, and it was nearly midnight. Not another soul graced the room but me. Listen, bathrooms are not scary ...

But they were on this night.

I was still alone when I reached the sink to wash my hands. It was an automated sink. Wave your hand over the electric eye you can never find, and the water comes on. As I stood at the sink in an empty bathroom, suddenly the flush of an automatic toilet roared behind me about three stalls down.

Whoooooooosssssshhhhh.

I found out I hadn't finished going to the bathroom after all.

I did what everyone does and bent over to look underneath the stall and see if anyone was there. The joint was empty. Toilets aren't scary ...

But they were on this night.

I got out of there before the kid from *The Shining* rolled down the hallway on his Big Wheel chanting, "Redrum! Redrum!" I bolted back into the theater, back to the safety of the seat next to my buddies. I watched the second half of the movie and deepened the scarring.

We headed home afterward in silence. I was still spooked when I looked over at Reagan. "So, what did you think of the movie?"

"Pretty good."

"Yeah. Me too."

I drove a little farther. Then I cleared my throat and spoke. "So, uh, Beth is out of town, right? She's at the girl's retreat, isn't she?"

"Yep."

"Well, you could, uh, you could stay at my house, if you want. Because Melanie is, you know, on the same trip. Plenty of space."

Reagan was like, "Ah, I don't kn—OK."

When we reached my house, we walked up the sidewalk to the front stoop. Now, I had no way of knowing a little family of birds had made a nest at the top of our porch. All I know is that when I stepped onto the darkened porch, they awoke. With a vengeance.

Birds flitted around our heads like something out of a Hitchcock thriller. It wasn't a bloodcurdling, terrifying moment, but it startled me enough to make me fumble my way through the door. Guess what? Birds are not scary . . .

But they were on this night.

Once inside the house, Reagan and I sat and talked. And we talked. We talked about as much stuff as possible. We talked about things that didn't matter — just stuff about stuff. After a while, we both knew we were stalling because we didn't want to be alone.

Our eyelids finally convinced our nerves to go to bed. I showed Reagan the guest room and then retired to my room, took off my jacket, and tossed it aside. I just oh-so-casually threw it.

Imagine this scene in slow motion.

As my jacket glided in midair, I walked toward the light switch that for some reason an evil builder had put on the other side of the room. I wasn't halfway across the darkened room when my jacket landed. How could I have known that my daughter, Zoe, had left her little doll in the chair? I had begun reaching for the light switch when the jacket landed on the doll, which then screamed, "Ha, ha, ha, ha! Let's play!"

Dolls aren't scary . . .

But they were on this night.

Let me tell you something. I flipped that light switch and bounced around my bedroom quoting Scripture. "God hath not given us the spirit of fear, but of power, and of love, and of a sound mind." "He will never leave you nor forsake you."

I belted out the chorus of a hymn. "Majesty, worship his majesty! Unto Jesus be all glory, power, and praise!"

Right then and there, I confessed everything I'd ever done and committed to a life of missions in the deepest, darkest outpost.

I just knew Reagan could hear me and thought I was losing it. Because I was.

Here's the thing. All the stuff that scared me—I put it there. I booted up the mental computer and loaded the file. And it's still there. It doesn't ever go away.

Dolls? They're still not cool. Any time, ever. When Zoe wants one for Christmas, my first question is whether it comes with batteries. If so, mark it off the list. You're supposed to play with dolls; dolls aren't supposed to play by themselves. Dolls that play by themselves are named Chucky, and that's a whole nother horror story.

I don't like to go into my basement now. Horror movies are to blame. I take Zoe with me. Zoe is ten.

"C'mon, Zoe. We have to get something out of Daddy's studio."

"Dad, we always have to get something together in the basement."

"You're my little helper."

"But Mom said it's time for bed."

"Hush and come on."

The point is this: The images we put into our brains matter. The music we pump into our heads matters. It's all going somewhere and eventually will come out, but it's never going away. I can go into a restaurant and hear a song from my high school years and tell you where I was when I heard it back in the day. I can tell you how the room smelled. It's seared into my brain.

It's amazing how scary movies can redefine reality and make us uneasy about things that never bothered us before. Toilets are not scary. Little kids' toys are not scary. Birds are not scary. But they all were redefined and became scary to me because of the effects of one movie.

This is why it is essential that believers saturate themselves in God's Word. When the world launches its multimedia salvos at us, we can overcome the trash with the purity and tranquility of God's truth. Digging into the truth helps us root out the weeds of the world.

Do you like to go swimming in the ocean at night? Anybody who has seen *Jaws* doesn't want to do that, even four decades after the movie debuted. Some people don't like swimming pools at night because of *Poltergeist*. Some folks don't like clowns because of Stephen King's *It*. Old dilapidated houses are automatically haunted because of *Psycho* and *Halloween*. Going into the basement in the dark is taboo because of most scary movies you've ever seen. In unsettling moments, we are convinced that things lurk under our beds and in our closets—all because movies have redefined how we see them.

Like the surprise twist in the worst kind of horror movie, that's exactly what the Enemy tries to do to your walk with Jesus.

Point to Remember

Satan works to redefine what we believe.

CHAPTER 8

NEW HEART, OLD MIND

In the same way that scary movies redefine routine circumstances and turn them spooky, the Enemy has redefined some things in our head.

Crafty and subtle, Satan takes the truth and tries to redefine it. For instance, in the most effective "gotcha" kind of way found in the best horror flicks, he's convinced a lot of believers that it's up to them to keep themselves saved and hold it all together. His approach works because such thinking is logical. It makes sense. We hold everything else in our lives together—or, at least on the surface, it looks like we do.

We keep our jobs by the way we perform. We keep good grades through our homework and study. We keep ourselves on the team through hard work and diligence. The way we live can make or break a lot of friendships. Or our marriage. In most areas of life, it makes sense to think we're the ones responsible for our success or failure.

Even though God's Word is the final authority on these matters, Satan somehow has convinced many people to believe they are responsible for earning their way to eternal life and heaven. Sadly, entire religions are based on works, and many of those folks who follow these religions will remain deceived until it's too late.

We hear God's Word speak truth into specific situations all the time. But by the time it bounces around our brains a few times and goes through the filters that Satan and his evil world system have slipped into our heads, we talk ourselves out of God's promises, provision, and protection. We convince ourselves that it's still all on our shoulders.

Let's aspire to let God have his Word back into our lives, so to speak. We need to dig deep to let him remind us of who he is and who we are now. We need to let him—and only him—define what we are responsible for and what we do with our lives.

Jesus isn't life enhancement. He's life. He alone is the way life works. You can't take my Jesus home with you. You can't take your pastor's Jesus home with you. Only your own walk with Jesus goes home with you. A relationship with Jesus is not automatic just because you walk into a building with a pretty steeple or one that is adorned with religious symbols. Buildings don't change your life. Songs don't change your life. They may change your mood, but the change lasts about as long as it takes for you to get back to the parking lot.

Sooner or later, we have to realize that Jesus is more than church. Consistent study of God's Word and consistent prayer are required to deepen our roots and redefine erroneous thinking. I like to use Romans 12:1 – 2 as a foundation:

> I appeal to you therefore, brothers, by the mercies of God, to present your bodies as a living sacrifice, holy and acceptable to God, which is your spiritual worship. Do not be conformed to this world, but be transformed by the renewal of your mind, that by testing you may discern what is the will of God, what is good and acceptable and perfect.

I disciple about sixteen of my high school students and twelve middle schoolers one-on-one every week. We talk and pray through a book of the Bible five or six verses at a time.

When we start a new study, we pause to check out a few background facts. We need to know the book's author, his audience, and his reason for writing. For instance, we know Paul wrote Romans. Right at the start of chapter 12, he writes, "I appeal to you therefore, brothers." So we know he's writing to fellow Christians. This means Paul told *Christians* to stop conforming to the pattern of this world. Guess what that means. It means Christians still conform to the world.

See, you thought you were the only hypocrite in the world. But Paul shows there were hypocrites way back then too. Even in the first century, with the church on fire and God shaking the world, believers blew it. They did just fine during a worship gathering, but as soon as the doors shut behind them, they faced an angry world. And they reacted like we react. They got stupid.

Paul told them to stop: "Don't let the world shape you. You're in the world, but you're not of it. Stop acting like you are."

But Paul doesn't stay in the negative. He doesn't just say, "Stop behaving that way." He also gets proactive. He tells them to focus on the one thing that will change their behavior fastest. He tells them to *renew their minds*.

This is a big deal. God's Word says I still need to be transformed *after* I've been transformed. My heart may be new, but my mind is still old. My thinking is still lost.

When we surrender to Christ, the spirit inside of us — the real person within the bag of bones we call a body — is renewed. Our brains are still flesh and blood that have recorded everything we've ever done. Our spirit is new, but we still have lost minds. Our brains become a battleground.

One minute we say, "If we confess our sins before God, he will forgive us and cleanse us from all unrighteousness."

The next minute, when we fail, we have a deep-seated fear. *I messed up again. God hates me.*

A little later we say, "I'm going to trust God with everything, give him all of me, and seek his kingdom."

Yet when the rough winds start to blow, we chew our nails and wonder, *Does God even know I'm here?*

This constant battle wages in our minds. We have to

counter Satan's attacks with God's Word. It's the only way to renew our minds under the torrent of attacks from the devil and the world he controls. Scripture calls him the prince of the power of the air (Ephesians 2:2), and I think of that title every time I think of airwaves. His multimedia assaults are relentless through cable, satellite, phone, Wi-Fi, and Internet signals.

Several years ago, I studied the armor of God in Ephesians 6. I thought about the belt of truth (God's Word that holds everything together), the breastplate of righteousness (to guard my heart), the shoes of the preparation of the gospel of peace (to share Christ everywhere), the helmet of salvation (to guard my mind), and the sword of the Spirit (God's Word, the only weapon I need). I noticed it all began and ended with God's Word. I also noticed that I needed protection for my heart and mind.

Then I thought about Philippians 2:12–13, where Paul tells us to work out our own salvation. A little ditty came to mind, and I have preached it ever since.

In the war of the mind, I will make my stand
In the battle of the heart and the battle of the hands.

Long before those words became the bridge to my song "Courageous," I hammered the saying into the heads of thousands of teenagers over several years. I used it to remind them why Romans tells us we need to renew our minds by diving into God's Word.

Have you ever sat in the middle of a prayer or worship time, only to have a really inappropriate scene from a movie or book or a nasty lyric from a song pop into your head? And you think, *How did that even get in my head right now?*

Let me phrase it another way. Have you ever been in the middle of a worship time or sermon and a nasty scene from a movie you *never* saw pop into your head? Of course not.

If you've been distracted by inappropriate imagery, how did it get there? You put it there when you willingly watched it in the first place.

We taint our minds with stuff we're trying not to do anymore. We iPod and iPad our brains to death with lifestyles that we don't live anymore because, even though we now have a new life, we're still fans of our old lifestyle.

The only way we will ever thrive is if we first are transformed by the renewal of our minds. So begins the battle of the heart and the battle of the hands.

Point to Remember

The only way to thrive is to be transformed by the renewal of our minds.

CHAPTER 9

THIS, THAT, AND THERE

Even though I've taught about the battle of the heart and the battle of the hands for years, I didn't realize until recently that each battle is a perfect fit for the Thrive concept.

The battle of the heart involves digging deep.

The battle of the hands involves reaching out.

When that Alabama farmer told me that the root system of the giant oak tree reaches beneath the earth as much as its limbs stretch into the sky, we walked away from the tree so I could get a wide angle for a photo. When we made our way back to the tree a few minutes later, Psalm 1 popped into my mind. I quoted it in chapter 2.

Now read the first sentence of the passage in the negative and see what happens.

Not blessed is the man
who walks in the counsel of the wicked.

If all of your counsel comes from the world, you're going down. That's when you find you're no longer walking but standing in the company of sinners, and the way you live confuses other people. They think, *I don't want anything to do with his God if that's what it means. It's no different from where I am right now.*

Now you're no longer even standing. You're sitting with the scoffers. You're in the middle of a church service picking apart everyone and everything, with your mind wrapped around everything but Christ.

It's a pattern. It's a slow fade.

You're not the first person Satan ever messed with. He made war with God. Figuring you out probably didn't take long. He knows just what buttons to push, and he keeps his fingers right there. He doesn't need to hit you with any new temptations. He's got your favorites on speed dial. He hits you with the same ones over and over and over until you feel like more and more and more of a failure.

After Jesus had fasted for forty days in the wilderness, Satan tempted even him. At Christ's physically weakest point, he still knew what to do. Every time Satan hit him with temptation, Jesus answered him with Scripture.

The battle of the heart requires digging in and establishing a vibrant root system. I have to hide God's Word in my heart so I don't sin against him. I have to guard my time with God every day because it's the first thing the Enemy attacks. He would much rather have you coast from church meeting to church meeting without engaging in the Lord. If you don't learn to feed yourself, you wind up dumpster diving for someone else's leftovers.

If we keep planting things into our old life, what will come out of us? Old life. We have to dig deep into our new life, and when we read God's Word, we hear his voice.

In the battle of the heart, I want to be so in tune with the Holy Spirit that I don't question whether I'm in step with Jesus. I know I am. Like a child who knows his mother is always near, I want to walk in the assurance of God's presence. I want temptation to stink in my nose. I want sin to sicken me rather than to woo me.

Galatians 6:7–8 is our GPS on how to get there: "Do not be deceived: God is not mocked, for whatever one sows, that will he also reap. For the one who sows to his own flesh will from the flesh reap corruption, but the one who sows to the Spirit will from the Spirit reap eternal life."

Why do we feel closer to the Lord after we spend only one hour at church on Sunday? Because we took the time to pour into our new life. What if that was a lifestyle rather than a trip to a building every week (or every other week)? All we did was pour into our new life and starve our old life. We closed out the world and the distractions and opened up his Word, and in just one hour our perspective changed.

This is an irrefutable principle: *When I sow to the Spirit, God's Spirit begins to change my thinking, my tastes, my will, my emotions.* This is how I learn to walk in the assurance of God's presence. This is how temptation that once enticed me now reeks to me.

When I wage the battle of the heart and pour into my new life, then new life will come out.

While the battle of the heart involves digging in and growing our roots on God's Word, the battle of the hands is how I refer to obedience. It's all about working out through our hands what God has worked into our hearts.

When we yield to Jesus, he works through us to reach others. We cannot produce fruit in and of ourselves any more than a detached tree limb lying on the ground can produce leaves.

I want my heart to be so close to God that I would never dream of surrendering in the battle of the hands. This means that sometimes, through a sheer act of my will, I'll choose to obey the Lord I love by refusing to go *there* or join in *that* or click on *this*.

All of us have our *this*, *that*, and *there*.

What you direct your hands to do reveals the condition of your heart. Your actions are the outward expression of an inner reality. If you were a tree, your heart would be your root system and your hands would be your branches.

At the end of Luke 6:45, Jesus says that out of the

abundance of the heart a person's mouth speaks. In the same way, out of the overflow of the heart our hands act and our feet move.

Now check out the context of that verse. Notice what Jesus uses as his first object lesson:

> "No good tree bears bad fruit, nor again does a bad tree bear good fruit, for each tree is known by its own fruit. For figs are not gathered from thornbushes, nor are grapes picked from a bramble bush. The good person out of the good treasure of his heart produces good, and the evil person out of his evil treasure produces evil, for out of the abundance of the heart his mouth speaks."
>
> *Luke 6:43–45*

I know my flighty heart. I know I can be the first guy to cave in to temptation. I do go there. I do jump into this. I do click on that. I do flip to that channel. How did I get there? How did my heart bend away from God when I seemed to be doing well? Because that's what hearts do. They're made of flesh.

Even though I try to guard my heart so it will stay bent toward God, I still need to set up some roadblocks that will help when my heart gets fickle and tries to pull away from the Lord.

You don't have to struggle with viewing inappropriate websites to know the Internet is a hazard. Sometimes all you have to do is check your e-mail, and you'll stumble across vile content in spam. It's out there, and Satan steers it straight to you. That's why we need wonderful aids like covenanteyes. com to serve as a roadblock against pornography and undesirable content.

Maybe porn isn't your issue. Your roadblocks may need to be against sales on handbags or against Pinterest posts on the latest and greatest furniture accessory. You may need to erect roadblocks in the gym to make sure you don't turn fitness into the pursuit of a body that becomes your idol. The Enemy knows your buttons. So put up roadblocks that prevent you from even going *there* in your thoughts.

Let's be willing to set up barriers. We all want to be able to say we did the right thing because our heart is right with God. But the truth is that sometimes we need to be safe — even when we do have an intimate walk with the Lord. It's not smart at any time to put good people in bad situations, because anything can happen. In fact, if you're like me, some of your biggest times of temptation come immediately on the heels of great blessings or mountaintop experiences with God.

The best roadblock is to have a friend to whom you give the right to get into your business. The arrangement, however, needs to be authentic. Don't play games. If you want it, mean it. Everyone wants an accountability partner until it's time to be held accountable. I've seen this before:

"Ask me anything you want."

One month later: "Oh, you're so holy to ask me that. Why are you so legalistic and judgmental?"

It helps to give godly friends permission to check our oil

and then be careful not to dismiss what they say. It's time to get smart and take the offensive. We have to jump on this battle and stop waiting for life to happen to us. Remember, we're supposed to be the hands and feet of Jesus. Let's fight to keep those hands pure so we can reach out and allow what's in our roots to seep out to impact others.

Point to Remember

The battle of the heart and hands
can strengthen our new life.

CHAPTER 10

THE FOURTH DISCIPLINE

The only chance to have success in our daily battle is to build a solid foundation. The only way to erect a foundation is to dig. Ask any builder — the taller the building, the deeper the workers have to go to dig the foundation.

A believer's foundation is his root system, and God has made a way for us to deepen our roots through the practice of spiritual disciplines. The Bible stresses the necessity of worship, prayer, and study of Scripture. Those are the Big Three essentials in growing as a believer. If we want to grow, we will embed these disciplines into our spiritual DNA.

A fourth discipline is often overlooked. While it may not

immediately come to mind as a discipline, an argument can be made that Jesus elevated it to be among his top priorities.

Community.

When I say community, I mean sharing life with other followers of Christ. Of all the Bible's descriptions of the church, perhaps none is more appropriate than "the body of Christ." Nothing better describes the church's nature and mission. If we're the body of Christ, then by nature we are a collection of individual parts grouped into a purposed whole. Time after time in God's Word, Jesus and the apostle John admonish believers to love each other. Check out John 13:34–35; 15:12, 17; 1 John 3:11, 23; 4:7, 11–12; and 2 John 5. In fact, Jesus said people will know who we are—that we actually belong to God and Jesus belongs to God the Father—by how we love (how we treat) each other (John 13:34–35; 17:20–21).

Community is a part of digging in your roots. If you're only a roots person, full of knowledge without any reach, you're useless. At the same time, if you dig in *alone*, not only are you useless as a reach person; you also don't have a good picture of God. God is community. Even in his essence, he is three Persons in one—Father, Son, and Holy Spirit—and they're always together.

Nicodemus came to Jesus by night and told him that his fellow Pharisees have been talking about him. "Rabbi, we know that you are a teacher come from God, for no one can do these signs that you do unless God is with him" (John 3:2).

I love how Jesus countered that statement. "Truly, truly,

I say to you, *we* speak of what *we* know, and bear witness to what *we* have seen, but you do not receive *our* testimony" (John 3:11, emphasis added).

Nicodemus tells Jesus "we know" about you. Jesus answers with an authoritative "*we* know" about you. He is speaking of the triune God — the Father, the Holy Spirit, and Jesus himself.

In John 5:19, Jesus says he can do nothing on his own but only what he sees the Father doing. He talks about sending the Helper, the Holy Spirit, in John 16:7–11. God is all about community.

By its very nature, the church is community (root word: *commune*). The collective whole is greater than the individual parts, but the individual parts are essential to the whole. God gave us spiritual gifts to complement each other (1 Corinthians 12). If we were meant to be Lone Rangers, God would have given us all the same gifts and passions.

Instead, one woman is creative and another is organized. One man speaks prophecy and another supplies mercy. So when we come together, we work together. In Matthew 5:14, Jesus says, "You are the light of the world. A city set a hill cannot be hidden." This suggests the concept that we shine brightest when we serve in community. It takes more than one person to make a bright city that cannot be hidden.

We are created for the express purpose of glorifying God by knowing him and making him known, and we come together under the Head — a connected body with arms, feet, hands, elbows, and armpits. Unfortunately, I've known a lot of armpits in my day, but most of the time it's all good.

Please don't skim over the verses about spiritual gifts in 1 Corinthians 12 in mechanical get-me-to-something-that-changes-my-life fashion. These verses will change our lives if we truly believe them. They are among Scripture's strongest argument for participating in regular church gatherings.

We either believe we are a small but essential part of the body of Christ or we don't. We either believe Jesus meant it when he called us to community or we don't.

Every time somebody tells you to go to church, they spit out some version of Hebrews 10:25: "Don't forsake the assembling of yourselves together." That's a good verse, but I hope we don't need a directive. If God calls his church the body of Christ, what other encouragement do we need to get together and stay together?

Jesus is God himself, and during his time on earth he didn't do ministry alone. He started the church by discipling a group of men. Similarly, we forfeit a significant part of our growth when we do not join with other believers.

Disclaimer: I know special circumstances can prevent people such as the sick, elderly, and shut-ins from gathering with fellow believers. God knows who you are and can grow you right where you are. He also knows your heart and whether you would gather with other believers if you could.

Why is community so important? Because one of the primary ways God ministers to us is through other believers. When Jesus was crucified, the disciples huddled in fear of the authorities. On the surface, it's easy to judge them in their weakness, even though every one of us would have trembled right there with them. But what is apparent in this picture is beautiful fellowship and community because of the trial they were enduring as a body. Fellowship is not pizza and Coke after church; it's the certainty that we're in something together and that our common faith will keep us going.

We have about four hundred teenagers involved in our student ministry at Eagle's Landing, and one guy cannot lead that many people the right way. You can't lead through position. You have to lead through relationship. So I have fifty of the most amazing adult workers you'll ever meet. They volunteer their time to love on kids, and not just on Sundays and Wednesdays. Youth ministry doesn't work that way. It doesn't stop at the doors of the church. It means texts in the middle of the night. It means phone calls on the weekend. It sometimes means getting in your car and picking up a teenager when they need a lift in more ways than one. These adult workers are gold.

For these workers to be leaders, they have to teach a small group. To teach a small group, they can't be in their own adult small group because all the small groups happen at the same time. One of the sweetest times I enjoy as a leader is every other Sunday night in our cafeteria. All of our adult workers get together for a bimonthly Bible study. That is our small group. That's our community.

We go around the table and tell stories about what God is doing in our ministry. We talk about the kids who are breaking our hearts. We talk about the ones who are starting to get it. And we talk about how God spoke to us as we prepared that week's lessons for the students. The first fifteen minutes are just for hanging out, talking, and being together. There's food on the table, but where we really feed each other is through our relationships. In fact, it has become one of my best sources of community — the place where I am fed.

This get-together doesn't have to be about some particular topic. Sometimes it's important just to be together and to love Jesus together. Sometimes it's essential to have other people with whom we share the same fellowship of suffering, because we're all banging our heads against the wall for some of these kids, and everybody else in the room feels the same way. We celebrate each other's victories and agonize over our defeats, and we lean on each other.

This group that meets every other Sunday night is the one group I can go to and not have to "be on." It's the one group I can just "be with." Do you have a group that you love to "be with"? Do you have any partners in the ministry?

Paul's letter to the Philippians is nicknamed the Book of Joy, even though he wrote it from prison. He tells God's holy people in Philippi, "You've been partners with me in the gospel from the first day until now. You've stuck with it and you've stuck with me." It honors God when we do something bigger than ourselves and need each other to do it. That won't just happen in a circle on Sunday morning. It's going to start there, but we need other believers to do life with us and undergird us through the hard stuff.

Even evangelists on the road alone, even missionaries in

the field alone, will say God doesn't talk to us only when we're alone in our quiet time. God talks to us all the time. He is called Wonderful Counselor for a reason. He doesn't just speak through hundred-year-old theology books. He'll also speak to you through twelve-year-old kids who will hit you between the eyes.

I recently attended a Student Leadership University conference in Orlando, where SLU vice president Brent Crowe talked about leading a teenage girl to Jesus. The girl wanted to tell him how she felt after she had surrendered to the Lord. He braced for some sappy emotionalism as he thought to himself, *She doesn't really have to tell me. I've done this a thousand times.* But he also wanted to make sure she understood what God had done in her life. So he waited to listen. Then she opened her mouth.

"You know that soft drink commercial where the drink machine is standing there and all of a sudden this big zipper comes down? And when it unzips everything comes off and there's a new soft drink machine there? That's how I feel."

Brent sat stunned. "Wow! That is perfect. That is exactly right."

Out of the mouths of babes ...

Through the body, through community and being around Pauls and Timothys, you dig deep into your spiritual roots. Timothy devoted his life to Jesus Christ through the ministry of the apostle Paul. The New Testament outlines how Paul discipled Timothy and continued to encourage and instruct him even after Timothy became the pastor of the church at Ephesus.

We all need some Pauls in our lives. Pauls are people who challenge us and earn the right with their lives to talk to us. They're further along spiritually than we are and have deeper roots than we do. Who are your Pauls?

We all need Timothys too. We need people to pour into. You'll be amazed what you learn from your Timothys. They bring a fresh perspective. They don't understand all the religious rules yet. They're running around and bumping their heads on life. But they often demonstrate more faith than we do because they really believe there's nothing God can't do. Like our kids, they'll regurgitate uncomfortable reminders like, "You said God can do anything, right?"

Just as God will use you as a Paul in someone's life, he'll also use your Timothys to help keep you focused on him and vibrant in ministry. One feeds off the other. One helps the other. Both love each other. All of it glorifies Jesus.

That's community.

Point to Remember

*Like Bible study, prayer, and worship,
community is a discipline.*

CHAPTER 11

THE GIFT

I stressed community in the last chapter because the church no longer stresses it enough. As much as technology and social media are supposed to create community, they more often leave us isolated behind a keyboard.

I realize we can't live with our church friends 24/7. But through the common interests of Bible study, worship, and prayer, we can always be there for each other.

Community is huge for me, and God has blessed me by allowing me to make my living leading group worship. My biggest worship time, however, comes when I'm alone in the car. Most of my songwriting time comes after worshiping God right there behind the wheel.

Worship is taking God's best and giving it back to him.

This can happen in serving, in giving, in singing, in admiring his majesty in creation. A butterfly can lead to tears of adoration for a holy God.

An attitude of worship is the vanguard of our hearts. The idea that citizens of Jerusalem placed palm branches on the ground and sang hosannas for five days before they screamed, "Crucify him!" shows how quickly we can focus on ourselves. Worship is not praising the God you want. It's praising the God who is. Worship is what we're created for, and we're never more at peace than when we're doing what we're created to do. Worship is God's gift to us, and through worship we enjoy fellowship with him (community!). But he didn't give us worship because we have to remind God of how good he is. He's God. He gave us worship as a gift so we can do what we're created to do.

I once performed a church skit with my wife. We staged the skit as if it were her birthday party. Melanie sat onstage, and I burst onto the scene and plopped next to her.

"Happy birthday, sweetie," I said. "This is *your* day! It's all about you. I've got presents."

I slid over three huge boxes, wrapped in bright paper and bows and full of tissue paper. Melanie acted overjoyed. In rehearsal, I had prompted her to tear off the paper and throw it all over the stage in excitement as she opened the boxes.

She reached inside the first box and pulled out a watch. A man's watch.

"Oh, hey—it's a watch," she said.

"Yeah, don't you love it?" I said. "It's awesome!"

"Um … it's kinda big."

"Nah, it's perfect. It's going to be just right."

"Is this a lady's watch?"

"No, silly." I fastened the watch on my wrist. "Now, can you imagine how you'll feel? I mean, I'd be so happy to wear this if it would make you happy. And this is all about you and about us being together and the magic and the beauty and the wonder of our relationship."

"Oh, OK," she said, a lilt in her voice.

"But there's more. Open this one," I said.

We went through the whole excitement routine again as she unpacked two other boxes. The first had a softball glove. Then she reached in the last box and pulled out a leather jacket. It was sleek and black, and the people in the front row could smell the new leather. Melanie let out a shrill giggle and stood to lift it to herself for sizing. Once again, her beaming face fell.

The jacket was extra-large. I grabbed it, put it on, and pranced around to model the perfect fit. I held up my arm to show the wristwatch as I raised my eyebrows and broke into a cheesy smile.

"This has been the best birthday you've ever had," I said. "C'mon, sweetie. We have some more surprises. Several other people out here have presents for them—I mean, for you too."

I ran off the stage and left Melanie standing in the middle of the shredded boxes and wads of paper. She looked out at the audience with a confused look, turned, and walked off the stage as the lights dimmed.

I came back onstage and looked out at the crowd.

"We're all here to worship Jesus today. Worship is giving back to God the best he's given us. It's a gift of praise and adoration of him," I said. "How do you think he sees our gifts? Were our gifts about him? Or was our worship really about us?"

A sign of spiritual maturity is when we show that we know the gift is to be given back. God is so awesome that even in a moment that is all about him, he pours everything out on us and fills us with a sense of his presence. May our hearts spill out such gratitude that we're never hesitant, never bashful, to lift our voices to praise him, as Romans 15:5–6 tells us: "May the God of endurance and encouragement grant you to live in such harmony with one another, in accord with Christ Jesus, that together you may with one voice glorify the God and Father of our Lord Jesus Christ."

This verse shows us that worship deepens our community with God and with fellow believers. But worship has another purpose that I didn't learn about until I became a student pastor. Worship teaches relationship and therefore teaches us how to pray.

Prayer is conversation. That's why I like to start prayer with worship, because worship is going to God without asking for anything. It's just praising God for who he is and thanking him for what he's done.

I heard a preacher say one time, "If you want to know how selfish you are, just start praying and see how long you can go without asking for anything." I frowned. A little pompous and determined to prove him wrong, I set out to pray with no petitions. I lasted maybe three, four sentences. I instinctively asked for something. I didn't know how not to ask.

When I first learned about the psalms, I understood them to be songs. That's what the word *psalms* means. It took me a while to realize that they were really prayers put to music. David and other writers of the psalms showed how worship and prayer correlate. And what does David do in the psalms? He opens his heart and dumps out everything to the Lord. He is unreserved. He is unashamed. He is transparent. He even asks God to destroy those who want to destroy him. David is *real*. I learned how to pray by studying the book of Psalms. It dawned on me that God wants us to converse with him because, as Psalm 25:14 makes clear, he is our friend.

When we talk with friends, it's not cool to tune them out or patronize them with mechanical dialogue. I'm guilty of doing that to God through rote prayers that sound more robotic than fervent. "God, thank you for today. Thank you for your mercy and your grace. Thank you for the food. Oh, wait, it's not mealtime." We can shift into rote prayers because we're just trying to get through the moment.

We all have a friend who seems to talk just to be talking,

and we spend a lot of effort trying to get away from that person. How often are we like that friend when we approach God? "Oh, blah, blah, blah. So anyway, here's what's going on."

On a few occasions, people who attended my Bible college at the same time I did have contacted me since Casting Crowns started releasing records and going out on tours. They had nothing to do with me early in my ministry career. I was in Daytona struggling as a young student pastor. I was at Eagle's Landing trying to figure out how to build a vibrant ministry in a big church. No one called to check in on me. But now that we're on the radio, everybody is my best buddy. They like to reminisce with me, over e-mail, for about three sentences.

"Hey, man, remember me from Bible college? Boy, what good times. Here's what I need. We're doing a little fund-raiser."

After that happened a few times, I thought to myself, *I don't really want people like that in my life.* Then one morning in prayer I realized I do the same thing to God.

A lot.

I'm glad he doesn't say, "I don't really want people like that in my life."

Regular prayer doesn't have to be rote or formulaic, and it certainly shouldn't be self-centered. I don't have those kinds of conversations with my wife, and I don't have to have them with my Creator. It's a friendship. It's community with God.

Our worship and how passionately we dive into the chance to connect with him do not make God stronger or weaker. Remember Tinker Bell from the children's classic story *Peter Pan*? Tinker Bell reappeared only after someone clapped hard and believed.

Our worship, our clapping real hard, and even our believing in God don't make him more or less of who he is. Our worship does, however, reveal who we are and what we believe about God. I also have my convictions about worship during a church service. It's easy to say that you can be quiet in public worship and not sing. I guess that could be the case for some introverts. Maybe. But if the Holy Spirit is in you, he's got to come out. It's your chance.

Philippians 2 tells us that at the name of Jesus every knee will bow and every tongue will confess that Jesus is Lord. I have a feeling that when all of those tongues confess, it's going to be loud. That's just a theory. I wouldn't want that scene in heaven to be the first time I praised his name in public. I wouldn't want to be a believer for much of my life and have the first time my tongue confesses in a great voice that Jesus is Lord be after my life is done.

I want to do it now.

Point to Remember

Worship deepens our community
with God and fellow believers.

CHAPTER 12

ALL ABOUT
THE HANG

One of the perks of serving as a student pastor is the frequency with which I get to accompany youth groups as they visit theme parks like Six Flags.

The funny thing about Six Flags is that what's on your mind going there and what's on your mind leaving is the same thing. You go in thinking about riding roller coasters, and when you're headed home, all you talk about are the rides you rode and the fun you had.

But what did you actually do for 90 percent of the time you were at Six Flags? You stood in line.

And the truth is, standing in line is a big part of why I go. To me, Six Flags is all about the hang. Sure, I want to ride as many rides as I can and be able to say I did it. Now, I don't like spinning rides—going in circles leaves me with bad issues that involve revisiting lunch. But roller coasters make me feel young again. Mostly, though, I want to be in line with as many kids as I can, moving at .005 miles per hour for hours at a time along those endless rails and just talking.

You talk about nothing — not schedules, not deadlines, not college majors. You're not looking for teaching moments. You just tune in and learn everything about the kids' families and friends and what they like—the concerts they go to, the songs on their iPod. You learn how they treat each other and who has heavy rivalries. You see a guy and a girl off to the side, and you realize a romance is emerging. You see a kid over on the next rail who is awkward and doesn't know how to interject at the right time. Another kid down the line is obnoxious just because nobody listens to him. You see all of these dynamics.

Nobody goes home talking about the line, but that's what we did all day.

So it is with Bible study.

A lot of times, when we tell stories about our spiritual lives, we focus on some big roller-coaster moment. But where do you really get to know Jesus? You get to him when you're in line. Every day as you pray, dig into his Word, go to work, go to school, sit at lunch, and drive home, you grow in Christ as you take time in your heart and mind to stand in line with the Lord.

The exhilarating roller-coaster moments serve only to show where we are with God. As much as we think the high points shape us, they only reveal how we've attended to our spiritual lives to that point. It's the same with our quiet times. We go into our quiet times wanting the earth to move. We want Billy Graham thunder to fall. We want to be able to say, "John Piper was in our church yesterday and dropped a bomb on us." But it's not about the roller-coaster ride anymore. It's just you and God, and you're not in it for the buzz of an emotional experience. Think about your best friend. You're not looking for an adventure every time you hang out with her. You just hang out and talk about nothing, and you're fine. Let's aspire to be so intimate with God.

Along with wanting the earth to move, another factor that can detract from our time with God is that we often go into it wanting a win. We want to take the problem of the day to the Lord and have it fixed now. The impatience of the American culture maims our walk with Jesus. We need to soak in God's Word, not so that something good will happen but so that we get to know him.

People tell me all the time that when they started having a quiet time, their week went so much better.

I tell them, "No, you probably had just as cruddy a week as you had before. It's just that *you* are different. You don't see the same. You don't hear the same. Your perspective is different. You dived into God's Word and grew closer to him, and now when you get out into the world, you see people for who they are. You understand you're just as broken as they are. You don't want to scream at them anymore. You just want to love on them."

Once again, we see the Romans 12:1–2 Effect. When we renew our minds through God's Word, everything gets redefined.

I don't dig into God's Word because I've got to. I dig in because I get to. I'm in his Word today because I want to know more about him and more about me. I can't emulate someone I don't know. When I open God's Word with a prayer on my lips and worship in my heart, that's when I commune with God. That's when I grow in Christ. That's when Bible study, prayer, worship, and community all come alive.

And whether I'm at the top of a roller coaster or worshiping out of the depths of God's Word, I can't help but raise my hands.

Point to Remember

Bible study is simply hanging out with God.

CHAPTER 13

MIGHTY MEN

For three years in college, I served as youth pastor at First Baptist Church of Samson, Alabama. It was the largest church in a small town, and I was shocked that they even knew my name to call me to minister.

The youth group had about twenty kids when I got there. One of the kids was Reagan Farris. You'll recall that I mentioned him earlier as the friend who spent the night at my place after we stupidly watched a horror movie together. He served for several years alongside me as co-student pastor here at Eagle's Landing and is now pastor of a church plant in New Orleans, Louisiana. But at the time I got my start as a youth pastor, he was a high schooler, and I didn't know him any better than any of the other kids in the group.

Not long after I started in my new role, I took the group to a youth conference where speaker Roger Glidewell shared the story of David and his mighty men in 2 Samuel 23. The account says, "These are the names of the mighty men" (verse 8), and it chronicles King David's thirty-seven men who were the most valiant soldiers for the army of Israel. Three men draw particular attention.

The first is Josheb-basshebeth. He was the chief of the three men and was famous for killing eight hundred enemy soldiers with his spear in one battle.

Next to him was Eleazar, who stood with David against the Philistines when the rest of Israel's fighters bailed. He fought so long and so hard that his hand froze to the sword. I love how the Bible says, "And the LORD brought about a great victory that day" (verse 10).

Shammah was the third mighty man. The Philistines had set up camp near a field of one of Israel's crops of lentils, and yet again the Israelites fled. Except for Shammah. He "took his stand ... and defended" the lentils from theft and struck down the Philistines. Once again, Scripture says, "The LORD worked a great victory" (verse 12).

Three men. Three courageous deeds that set them apart for posterity.

One of their most amazing feats comes when David and his army are besieged in a cave as the Philistine army runs roughshod over Bethlehem, David's hometown. His heart aches for his fellow villagers as the standoff wears on for days. While hidden, David and his band of misfits plot their next move. In his tired, homesick grumblings, David says aloud, "Oh, that someone would give me water to drink from the well of Bethlehem that is by the gate!" (verse 15).

The mighty men give each other glances that need no words.

"You ready?"

They fight through the lines, go to the well, draw a cup of water, fight back through the lines, and go to David. "Here is your water, sir."

At the youth conference, Roger told this story with passion and then brought his voice low for his closing point. He looked out over a roomful of kids and left them with one question. "What if," he said, "there were mighty men and women for God in our cities?"

Our students went home wide-eyed.

Along with Reagan, I had three other ninth-grade guys named Jack, Rory, and Brent (not their real names). I remember the night we returned from the conference. We gathered to pray before going home.

By this time, our youth group had grown to about twenty-five students. The upperclassmen were the cool kids, so cool that they showed little spiritual leadership. The small band of freshmen comprised the serious students who wanted to pray.

We gathered in a circle near the door to the gym and held hands as they started praying for friends. Right in the middle of it, little backwoods Brent, the smallest guy in the circle, said, "Lord, we just want to be mighty men for you."

I got an idea and waited for the word "Amen."

"Guys, I think I'm looking at the mighty men of this city," I said. "You guys think you need to be older, bigger, and more mature, but I'm telling you, I'm looking at the mighty men right now."

I suggested we gather again the next day and pray for their school. They spoke at the same time. "All right!"

We met at 7:00 a.m. on the front steps of the church right on Main Street. As cars whizzed by, we sat and prayed that God would give us boldness to do something for him. I was brand-new in ministry and had no idea what I was doing. All I knew was that I loved God and I kind of liked these kids. I was just settling in and still trying to figure out my own daily quiet time.

That day marked the beginning of our regular morning prayer meetings, and almost immediately we heard results of the courage they fueled. The boys started sharing the gospel at school, and students responded. Within just a few days, Reagan came back and startled everyone. "I just led Brad Smith to Jesus."

Brad was a gang member who played on the high school basketball team. But Brad didn't quit the team to live for Jesus. He took Jesus to the team, and the influence of the Mighty Men grew.

Reagan, Jack, Rory, and Brent started going one by one to their friends and sharing the love of Jesus. They didn't try to argue people into heaven during the middle of a science class discussion on evolution. They weren't debaters. But when the opportunity arose, they asked questions and didn't embarrass people.

The results were promising as several kids gave their hearts to Jesus through the work of the Mighty Men.

And then it happened.

One morning I arrived at our prayer time and sensed a negative vibe. The boys were sitting on the steps in front of the church. They all stared at the ground. No one said a word. As I approached from the parking lot, I could feel the weight.

"Hey, guys. How's it going?" I said. "Everybody good?"

"Yeah, yeah, we're good."

A lot of empty nods. They were the Mighty Men. They thought they were always supposed to be good. I glanced at all four boys.

"Guys, what's going on?"

One by one, they started talking.

"I was at the end of my last class at school yesterday, and the teacher said something," Brent said. "I had my Bible with me, and I wrote a verse, and she made fun of me in front of the whole class."

He finally looked up with a long face. He didn't have to finish the story. I could tell he had not answered the teacher's mocking because he didn't know what to say.

"We're the good guys ..." he said, voice trailing off.

Reagan spoke next.

"My Paw Paw is dying." He had to choke back tears. His war-hero grandfather, who also had been his household's hero, was near death. Reagan was close to Paw Paw. How do you share Jesus from the heart when it's deflated?

I hadn't noticed Jack's face until he finally lifted his head. I saw one of his eyes had swollen almost shut. His infected eye was a mess.

This group of ninth graders poured out their hearts about all of these inexplicable roadblocks they had hit, and their eyes looked at me with an unspoken question.

"What are we going to do?"

On top of their woes, I had endured a brutal week at school and work. I had damaged my vocal chords, and my doctor had discouraged me from talking and had forbidden me from singing. So I had lost a chance to sing a solo at the Florida Baptist Convention. I'd had to stand offstage and watch another guy sing my song.

I wasn't exactly a student ministry veteran at this point. I wasn't much of anything. I was a college kid with a new wife and new life. Still, somehow at that moment God slipped his glasses on my eyes and put a guard over my mouth so I didn't say anything stupid.

The boys' heads were still down and their shoulders still slumped, and I was as surprised as they were to hear the words that tumbled out of my mouth. "Do you guys see what's happening here?" I said. "We come together to take a stand for Jesus and love on all of our friends, and what are the chances that all of us are going through something difficult at the same time? This isn't coincidence. This is spiritual."

I'll share what happened to the Mighty Men in chapter 15. But first, let's check out how all of us are susceptible to wanting to give up through fear and frustration — even one of Jesus' closest friends.

The Mighty Men were ready to give up too. Right then, on those front steps beside Main Street, the Lord moved and gave me the words to say. I'll never forget how those kids responded. They finally looked up from the ground and one by one began to nod, jaws set. They sensed, correctly, that God was about to breathe into the Mighty Men anew.

Point to Remember

When we start to thrive in the Lord, we will face opposition.

CHAPTER 14

THIS IS NOW

After Jesus' resurrection, Peter and the disciples see him. They actually see him. Not his spirit, not his apparition. They see him in the body and fully alive. They're sitting right there in the room when Jesus tells Thomas to reach out and feel the holes in his hands and side.

One of my favorite moments in Scripture is how Thomas responds.

This is the guy who had doubted when the other disciples said Jesus had already appeared to them once. Yet when Jesus appears a second time to the disciples with Thomas present, Thomas does not reach out and rub an index finger around the rim of a nail hole and say, "Oh, look at that wound!"

Instead, the only reaction Thomas can muster is spontaneous. "My Lord and my God!" (John 20:28).

Chill bumps.

Yet just a few days after watching this scene, Peter turns to some of the same guys and says, "I am going fishing" (John 21:3). I went away for a while on that verse when I first read it.

How do you just go fishing, with the resurrected Jesus popping in and out? Peter had not fished since the biggest payday of his career. In Luke 5, we read of Peter toiling all night without catching anything when Jesus tells him to try again. Peter is skeptical, but he does it anyway because that's what fishermen do. They hope beyond hope and get superstitious. Jesus gets supernatural. Peter catches so many fish that the nets start to snap.

That day, Peter leaves his nets and follows Jesus into ministry.

Peter never could have imagined what happens next. The blind receive sight. The deaf hear the voices of loved ones. The lame walk. The mute speak. The dead breathe again. People with leprosy — the nastiest, stinkiest, most contagious outcasts of society — see their skin restored. We don't even know what real leprosy looks like in America. Back then, noses fell off people's faces.

People from all around want to follow this man with whom Peter gets to spend all of his time. He sleeps beside him. He eats beside him. He laughs and jokes and cuts up with him. He realizes this man is the Christ.

In Matthew 16:13–20, when everybody else tries to guess aloud who Jesus really is, Peter is the only one who steps up with boldness and understanding when Jesus asks, "Who do you say that I am?"

"You are the Christ," Peter says, "the Son of the living God."

Jesus, the God-Man, looks at Peter and says, "On this rock [that is, on the truth you just pronounced] I will build my church, and the gates of hell shall not prevail against it."

Can you imagine Peter's reaction? He probably turned off to the side, pumped his fist, and said under his breath, "Yes!"

John and Andrew and the other guys probably looked down at the ground and muttered, "Stupid. I'm so stupid. I said Elijah. Really? Elijah?"

Peter got to do things no one else got to do, or maybe just one or two others got to do. He got to walk on water. He got to see Jesus transfigured. He got to drive out demons in Christ's name. He was the obvious leader of the disciples, the first one mentioned in all the lists of their names. He got to do all the cool stuff.

But when Jesus was on trial and the Jewish leaders started looking for the disciples, the first one people singled out was Peter. He denied Christ three times in a matter of minutes, just as Christ had foretold. While Jesus was being beaten, spit on, tossed around, mocked, taunted, and questioned, Peter cowered before a teenage girl who recognized him as a friend of the guy they were pummeling inside.

Peter got scared, because that's what people do. We're weak. As long as we have this skin on, we'll do some of the dumbest things imaginable.

In that one moment, when all eyes were on him, Peter choked. Three times. The last of the three times he even called down curses on himself.

One of the Gospels says that Jesus looked at Peter. Peter was on one side of the yard trying to run away as guards dragged Jesus from one building to the next, and their eyes met (Luke 22:61).

What did Jesus' eyes say? I'm certain he did not give Peter a look of scorn, condemnation, or contempt. I think his eyes wept for Peter. I think he pitied this man who was so full of human limitations.

I can't even imagine how Peter felt at this.

Or can I?

On a smaller scale, I've had that moment. I've drifted plenty of times. I've been out in the world and doing my own thing for my own purposes, knowing all along I was wrong. I've wondered to myself, *How did I ever get this numb? How did I ever get this far away and do the thing I just did? Good gracious, I remember when I prayed and cried down at the altar, and I was headed to China as a missionary for the rest of my life. And now I'm a mess and doing stupid stuff.*

Then I went to church and wanted to worship again, but all I could think about were the dumb things I'd done and the guilt on my head. I tried to sing songs about a holy, holy God, but all I could think about was unholy, unholy me. That's a nasty place to live.

When I fail, the Enemy lies to me. He wants me to remain a failure. "Are you sure you're even saved? Look at what you're doing."

He wants me out of the Word and into the mirror. If Satan can get me out of the Word to focus on my circumstances and on myself, he can mire me in numbing guilt and neutralize me. I recognize that, despite trying to live for Jesus, I've failed badly. Before long, I decide, *Oh, well. I guess that was my shot.*

But God is always faithful. He's always waiting on the shore, calling out to me.

I may have tripped a thousand times and stumbled back into church, but every time, Jesus has waited on me. A song hit me. A verse pierced me. A prayer crushed my heart. In some way, God spoke to his wayward child, and it was like Jesus locked eyes with me. All I could do was think, *What am I doing?*

I believe this is the explanation for Peter's fishing trip in John 21.

Remember, at this point the risen Christ has appeared to Peter one-on-one and then appeared at least two other times to the disciples in hiding. So at this point Peter has seen him three times.

For a while, I asked myself why Peter wanted to go back to fishing. It seemed odd. Then I remembered the scene where Jesus turned and caught Peter's gaze after his third denial. In that moment, I believe Peter thought, *That was my shot. I just blew everything.*

I think Peter numbed out. I think he checked out on life. I think even three appearances of the risen Jesus didn't shake him from the suffocating guilt of going back on his own word and denying Jesus not once, not twice, but three times. I think Peter went back to the only thing he thought he was worthy of—his old life.

Just when we're starting to thrive, the Enemy will try to derail us. He'll throw our past at us. He'll bring obstacles right now. He'll make us doubt our future. He'll even make us doubt whether all of this is real and whether we really belong to God. Sometimes, just like the freshmen who became known as the Mighty Men, we'll want to quit. Jesus always comes looking for us.

In John 21, Peter and a few of his disciple buddies are back on the water for the first time in about three years when a man on the shore yells out, "Hey, have you guys caught anything?"

"No, we haven't caught anything all night."

"Well, cast on the other side, and you might find something."

Peter hauls in the second biggest payday of his career. Once again, he leaves it behind, jumps in the water, and swims a hundred yards to get to Jesus again.

What Jesus began with his compassionate eyes after Peter

betrayed him, he finishes on the shores of Galilee with a beautiful restoration of his guilt-ridden friend. That's why I wrote a song called "This Is Now." It reminds us that John 21 is what Jesus does for all of us.

> *Just when I thought my sin had closed the door*
> *I see my Savior standing on the shore*
> *With arms wide open*
> *Just like the first time*
> *You called my name*

Even when we do the worst we can possibly do, Jesus catches our gaze. And he says, "You don't have to start again *for* me; I'll start over *with* you."

Point to Remember

Even when we stumble, Jesus is always ready to begin again.

CHAPTER 15

CLOSING LINE

Reagan, Jack, Rory, and Brent fixed their eyes on me as we sat on the church steps that difficult morning. They had made too much progress, surrendered too much pride, and risked rejection much too often to let a few hardships discourage them.

"Guys, this is bigger than us," I said. "God is doing something in this town, and the Enemy is coming after us. The cool thing is that God is bigger than all of this stuff, and it's actually all a part of his plan. Hang in there."

I turned to the New Testament to help make my points. For the first time in my life, I had been teaching students about the adversities of both Peter and the apostle Paul. God prompted me to use those Scriptures because I'd been reading them every night. So I reminded the Mighty Men of how Peter faltered and how Jesus restored him. Then I brought up Paul.

"Remember when Paul got saved and started his ministry? Remember what happened? The disciples wouldn't hang out with him. Only Barnabas would have anything to do with him, and Barnabas had to talk other believers into letting Paul hang out with them. The others in the church were scared to death of him. That was his chance to bail. And this is ours. Paul didn't bail, and neither will we."

That day, we prayed for a while, and everybody left with a renewed confidence. I sensed they realized, *We're doing something eternal here, something that matters. And we're in.*

They went back to school and continued to love on their friends. More kids accepted Christ. More joined our youth group. Later that year, Reagan plopped into the chair in front of my desk. What he said caught me off guard. "We're going to put on an assembly in the gym and share the gospel with our whole school."

"Awesome, man," I said, not wanting to discourage the poor, ignorant kids with their grandiose ideas.

"We've got a plan," he said. "We have the whole program figured out. I'm going to read this Scripture, and someone else is going to give his testimony, and at the very end we're going to share the gospel. It's going to be awesome."

There I was, at the end of my faith in what God can do. This assembly, this sweet little idea, was against school rules. It was against federal rules. I was scared for God. I thought,

*How do I encourage them to go forward? This is the real world.
This isn't an eye infection. This is the government. You can't
just do this.*

That's what I thought. What I said was something else.
"Well, what do we do next?"

They went to their principal, told him their plan, and
asked for the assembly. I looked forward to the relief of
the principal saying no. They had been living out loud for
Jesus for a while, and almost everyone in school knew that
these kids were all about Jesus. It wasn't a preacher doing
it. It wasn't a youth pastor. Everybody knew me because I
joined the Mighty Men for lunch in the school lunchroom.
But no one ever said, "Boy, that youth pastor over there is
really stirring things up." Even the older kids in our youth
group didn't know how to react to the Mighty Men. They
shrugged them off because they knew they should have done
it themselves but hadn't. But surely the Mighty Men had
overreached at last.

I waited for the principal to reject their plan for an
assembly.

Reagan walked up to me a few days later. "We're in," he
said. "They say we can do it. By the way, can you and your
band come play?"

"Wait. What?"

I was a member of a college quartet called One Voice.
We sang at churches and various events, and I had started
writing songs. Now the Mighty Men had pulled me and my
singing group into this assembly thing, and I was scared to

death. Was I going to be arrested? Would the FBI storm the place?

It wasn't long before I stood in the gym at Samson High School for a come-if-you-want assembly. Who doesn't want to get out of class? The place was packed.

One Voice opened with three songs and got out of the way of the Mighty Men. The kids performed skits and acted out a song about God's forgiveness. After a few testimonies, Reagan preached the gospel. I still remember his closing line: "You can be saved right now."

Sixty kids responded.

The next year, when the assembly was repeated, sixty-five kids accepted Christ.

And sixty-five more the year after that.

One year, Reagan witnessed to his baseball coach in the locker room. The coach surprised Reagan by visiting our church soon thereafter. He responded to the invitation and asked Jesus to change him. He is now a pastor.

A new principal and stricter policies were in place for the Mighty Men's senior year, and only about a dozen kids gave their hearts to Jesus. But still, all told, God changed the lives of more than two hundred kids during those four years.

It all started with guys who got saved and dug in their roots. Yes, they got attacked. But because of their roots, they stood strong.

That was then.

As I've said, Reagan pastors his own church now. But there's more. Rory is a pastor in Alabama. Jack is a rocking youth pastor in Enterprise, Alabama. Another kid who joined the group later, Wayne, is also a pastor.

This is now.

Point to Remember

God's mighty men and women respond to adversity by showing their strong roots.

CHAPTER 16

ALL YOU EVER WANTED

One truth we believers often have to learn the hard way is that the first thing the Enemy goes after is our time with God. It's basic military strategy—cut off communication, and all the ants run around and don't know what to do.

When I was a kid, my dad would make us watch Westerns with him. I'd be in the middle of Bugs Bunny, and during a commercial he would turn the channel to a Western and say, "This is a classic, son. It's a classic!" I'd have to sit there and watch it, which I hated at the time.

Usually it was a movie about cowboys and Indians. Dad would say the same thing every time. "All they gotta do is kill that Indian chief. If they can cut down that chief, it's all over because nobody will know what to do."

Satan wants to go after our communication with God to make us useless. We scurry into all manner of trouble when we don't hear God's voice. I've seen it in my own life. I see how I thrive when I dig my roots deep and draw from Jesus on a regular basis, and I see how I dive when I don't.

When I stop communicating with God, life tends to get a little grayer. I start living off my gut and using my own common sense and instincts to make decisions, and black-and-white turns to gray. The next thing I know, I'm thinking things I never thought, saying things I never say, and doing things I never do. Then life slaps me upside the head and I realize my slow fade with my own unspoken question. *What just happened?*

That's where one of my latest songs starts. "All You Ever Wanted" is about the guy who wakes up at the bottom of his Psalm 1 slow fade (walking to standing to sitting). The first verse describes him rousing from his Conceit Coma:

I just looked up today
And realized how far away I am from where you are
You gave me life worth dying for
But between the altar and the door
I bought the lies that promise more
Now here I go again

That last line points to the cycle that all believers experience at some point — failure, conviction, and remorse. Hopefully it leads to repentance. At these times I have to remind myself of the difference between false guilt and God's conviction. Satan throws guilt at us to tell us we're the worst Christian and biggest hypocrite ever. The Lord gently convicts us of a particular sin, maybe using a particular Scripture, and in his kindness he leads us to repentance. Godly sorrow produces repentance (2 Corinthians 7:10).

We fail because we take a God-given need and try to fill it with the world's answer. That's what sin is. We most often trip over our wants—the want to be loved, the want to be needed, the want to matter. We can boil down most of our sins into one of three areas—the lust of the flesh, the lust of the eyes, and the pride of life (1 John 2:16).

Satan tempted Jesus with these same allures in the wilderness.

He tried the lust of the flesh: "Aren't you hungry?"

He tried the lust of the eyes: "I'll give you everything you see."

He tried the pride of life: "If you're the Son of God, get your Father to send his angels to rescue you."

It's the same three approaches. It's all he's ever had.

Jesus answers him every time with Scripture:

- "Man shall not live by bread alone, but by every word that comes from the mouth of God" (Matthew 4:4).
- "You shall worship the Lord your God and him only shall you serve" (verse 10).
- "You shall not put the Lord your God to the test" (verse 7).

Just as he did with Jesus, Satan sees our legitimate needs and perverts them. "If you'll just meet them with this short-cut, you'll be happy."

I start to listen to his coaxes when I've allowed him to rob me of my time with God. Just when I'm a little off balance and he throws me yet another storm, my grayed-out think-ing can turn me sideways long enough to where I'll make a bad decision. I'll choose the world's path to meet God-given needs in my life.

Notice that I wrote that our needs are *God-given*. We usu-ally only attribute things we consider to be "good" as God-given. Talents are God-given. Bodily attributes (strength, beauty, athleticism, and so on) are God-given. We seldom consider that God gave us our needs—but he did. In fact, they're gifts. It is a gift to want to be loved. Why else would we pursue and give love? It's a gift to want to be needed. Why else would we reach out to others or fill voids? It's a gift to feel the need for significance. Why else would we pursue excellence and God's plan for our lives?

Yet we sabotage God's intentions to meet our needs when we pursue our own answers and the world's shortcuts.

I wrote "All You Ever Wanted" as an answer to this cycle. We learned earlier that Peter checked out, almost for good. But this song examines another angle, one we all know well. It's about the guy who thinks he can come out of the slow fade through his own efforts.

When we fall, we finally wake up and say, "Oh, man, what just happened?" Now that we've drifted from spending time in God's Word, the biggest influence on our minds is the world and not the Word. We're not being renewed. We're being re-olded. We're letting the Enemy define what fulfills us, and once again we resort to lost thinking on how to turn it around.

So how do we fix this? We think God is mad at us, so we shrink back from being transparent with him. That's when our brains reboot to the old way of thinking:

Well, what was I doing before when I was intimate with him? For one, I was going to church.

"OK, I'll do it. I'll go even more often."

I also belted it out during worship.

"You thought I was singing then? Wait till you hear me on Sunday. I'm going to be rocking."

I served in all kinds of outreach.

"That was nothing. I'm going to feed every homeless person in the city ..."

We take the things we were doing *because* God loved us, and now we do them *so* God will love us. The problem is that they don't go anywhere because we're doing them in our own power.

We're not down here trying to live holy lives so God will love us. We're trying to live holy lives because he loved us before we even knew the definition of holy. Somehow that got redefined when the Enemy snuck in and started asking questions that seemed logical. "Did God really say that?" That was his only question to Eve, and he used the same attack against Jesus. "God said he was going to do this, right? He said he'd give his angels charge over you and protect you. Let's test him."

Ever so craftily, with great subtleness, Satan attempts to alter truth and mute our ears to God. He makes perfect sense from a human perspective. We become a gerbil on the spiritual wheel: "I'm not doing this spiritual thing good enough. I have to do it better. But now that I'm living around a bunch of Christians, I can't act like I have problems, so I don't want to tell anybody."

I've been there before, so I know firsthand that these feelings and motives are sincere. We all want to be joyful. We don't want to seem like we're not doing well. We may be a church leader. Maybe we're teaching or singing in the choir. Maybe we're trying to be a good spouse or parent. Sometimes we think we can fake it until we make it. Maybe we can do this checklist as a jump start to get us to God.

But flesh never got us to God in the first place; flesh will never keep us with God; and flesh will never make any of this work.

Lord, I know I let you down
But somehow I'll make you proud
I'll turn this sinking ship around
And make it back to you
But all my deeds and my good name
Are just dirty rags that tear and strain
To cover all my guilty stains
That you've already washed away

That's the second half of the first verse of "All You Ever Wanted." My guy in the song is starting to grasp the truth. It takes him a while because he's like the rest of us. At last he has awakened from the slow fade, but instead of looking in the Word, he first looks in the mirror. When he looks in the mirror, he wants to fix the problem himself. When he finally looks in the Word, he sees that God already has fixed him.

The song's chorus offers the only solution to the mistake of trying to right our own wrongs and climb our way back to God. We don't have to climb anywhere. We have only to look up.

Freedom's arms are open
My chains have all been broken
Relentless love has called me from the start
All you ever wanted was my heart

Point to Remember

We can't fix our messes; all God wants is our hearts.

CHAPTER 17

TRYING JESUS

Whenever I share the gospel or talk to people about Jesus, one of the saddest and most frequent responses comes with a tone of resignation.

"I tried that."

I hear this from a lot of people who say, "I remember back when . . ." and then tell a story. It goes something like this: "I was struggling and I knew I was going the wrong way. I also knew God was the only one who could fix it, and I gave it all to him that day. But I just couldn't keep it going."

The longer I work in ministry, the more I hear the same claims:

"I tried Jesus. It didn't work."

"I couldn't hold on."

"I lost the fire."

"I blew it."

"I've failed too many times."

"I've done too many things."

It's amazing what grammar and word choice reveal. "I tried Jesus. It didn't work." Jesus isn't an "it." He's a he. "It" didn't work, because "it" is religion.

I look at them and gently shake my head. "You cannot *try* Jesus. It's impossible," I say. "Jesus is not a sweater. He's not a diet. He's not a behavior system. If you're going to *try* Jesus, the closest you'll ever get is religion, and religion is the stuff of God without God in it. It's the shell."

In Matthew 13, Jesus uses a parable to press home the importance of digging deep to establish roots. He tells of a sower whose seed fell along the path, on rocky ground, and among thorns. Each time, the seed fails to produce for different reasons. However, some seed falls on good ground and produces in various degrees of abundance. Jesus compares the seed that flourishes to the person who hears the Word of God and understands. He is the one who believes.

The New Testament is written in Greek. The Greek definition of the word *believe* means "to trust in Jesus in such a way that you place all of your weight on him." You count on him to hold you up. So there is no such thing as *trying* Jesus. We either yield our lives to him or we don't.

It's as if people look for a quick fix and think, *I'm going to go hear about what Jesus people do and try that. I realize I've gone the wrong way, so after I learn what the Jesus people do, I'll try to get good and come back.*

We need to be prepared to tell them it's too late to get good. Once we sin, we cannot unbreak the chain in our own power.

God demonstrated his love for us in that while we were still sinners, Christ died for us (Romans 5:8). So he's not waiting on us to get good. He knew what he was getting into long before we realized we needed him. He knew that we were lost, broken, and fallen and that we had no way back to him on our own. If we were able to do that, Jesus wasted a lot of suffering.

To the contrary, God says, "I will make the way back to me. I love you that much. I'm going to make the way with my Son. He is going to die your death. He is going to pay your debt, and he is going to take your place."

Belonging to Jesus isn't going out and being better. It's not living a holy life so he'll love you. Being a believer is just that — believing. It means confessing with your mouth that Jesus is Lord and believing in your heart that God raised him from the dead (Romans 10:9).

I talk about that verse a lot because we've said it so often that we almost ignore it. But it's the crux of the gospel. It's a life-giving verse!

The word *Lord* means "Ruler" or "King." I confess with my mouth ("confess" in the verse is present tense, meaning I'm continually confessing with my life) that Jesus is the Lord and King of my life.

You can't say no to the Lord, because he *is* Lord. This begs the question: Is Jesus my Lord? To confess with your mouth that Jesus is Lord is not to repeat a line in a dark worship center or slip up your hand during an invitation on a Sunday morning. Rather, it means we say in earnest, "You're the King of my life forever. I'm handing over some things right here by saying this. I'm handing over my future. I'm handing over my past. I'm handing over the controls here and now."

Romans 10:9 has been rendered as poetry by too many people. It's more than a pretty statement. It means inviting the resurrected Son of God to take over your life. He must increase. You must decrease. It means believing (trusting, placing your weight on) the truth that the same God who raised Jesus from the dead can raise you from the dead.

Second Corinthians 5:14 – 15 (NKJV) reads, "The love of Christ compels us, because we judge thus: that if One died for all, then all died; and He died for all, that those who live should live no longer for themselves, but for Him who died for them and rose again."

May our words and deeds confess Jesus to others. Let's show people we belong to him, with no ambiguity in our lives. Remember the symmetry of the roots and branches of the giant tree? Our reach will go only as far as our roots allow.

"I tried Jesus. It didn't work."

Our lives are a confession of what we believe and on whom we place our weight. Do we trust in Jesus, or do we trust in ourselves? Have we cultivated roots in Christ, or are we still playing religious games? I wrote this chapter to help us take a look at ourselves and check our own oil. Do our hearts truly belong to God? If they do, then it will be obvious. We will be willing to let him have all of us—for the benefit of others and for his glory.

The world is dead in its trespasses. You can't thrive if you're dead. First must come actual life. We know the Author of life, and he commands that we share him with others. All the excuses listed at the beginning of this chapter are why it's time for us to concentrate on putting our roots to good use and start reaching out.

Point to Remember

*As we give our lives to Jesus, we will reach out
and share him with others.*

PART 2
REACHING OUT

CHAPTER 18

LIGHTEST WHISPERS

In my second year on staff at a church near Atlanta in the mid-1990s, I invited a fellow youth pastor and his students to join us for worship and Bible study one night. I wanted him to see the product of disciplined ministry.

Our youth group was serious. In fact, we were beyond serious. We were studious. I would stand up to speak and announce the Bible passage of the night, and you could hear the pages turning. I was so proud of our very serious, biblical, awesome, humble youth group.

Knowing the depth of my disciples, I anticipated that the visiting youth pastor would approach me after the service and say, "Brother, teach me your ways. How have you done this?" I couldn't wait.

Well, the day came, and I was not disappointed in my group. We had our worship time, and every hand in the room reached high as they worshiped. When it came time to read, everyone focused on the Scripture. Few kids said a word, even in the back of the room.

Sure enough, after the service, the visiting youth pastor made his way to me. I'll call him Ron.

"Man, great night with your youth group," Ron said. "We had a great time."

"Yeah, well, we're a pretty focused group," I said with an exaggerated nod. "We really like to get into the Word, and we have a close bond."

He had one question. I was not ready for it.

"Yeah, it's a great group," he said. "Um—where are the lost kids?"

I stared into space.

I thought, *Oh, my goodness. We have a lopsided youth group.* No one from the world was showing up, which meant we weren't reaching a soul. We were so deep into the Word that we weren't reaching out at all. I discovered the hard way that we can nurture one area to the exclusion of another.

The maturing follower of Christ strikes a balance between pouring into his or her roots and reaching out to others.

Colossians 2:6–7 states, "As you received Christ Jesus the Lord, so walk in him, *rooted* and built up in him and established in the faith, just as you were taught, *abounding in thanksgiving*" (emphasis added). Here is scriptural proof that we must be rooted to thrive.

Our faith is rooted when we're planted by the constant living water of God's Word and prayer, providing us with stability and strength. But what does it mean to abound in thanksgiving? While it obviously means to be grateful, the word *abound* carries the connotation of action.

Abound is the verb form of *abundantly*, the word Jesus uses in John 10:10 to describe the thriving life he intends for us. To abound in thanksgiving is to purposely direct the overflow of our root system into other people's lives.

The only fruitful Christian is the one who abides (hangs in there) with Jesus. We can't abound (thrive) unless we abide in Christ. When we do, he produces the fruit. We can reach out in a million and one ways. We hear him in his Word; we sense the Holy Spirit's nudges; and we move. This is what it means to reach out. It essentially means to obey. The Bible says that to obey is better than sacrifice (1 Samuel 15:22). We can offer ourselves in the grandest ways, make noble sacrifices, and still please God less than we do when we yield to his lightest whispers.

Approach that hurting girl in the next booth and tell her about Jesus.

Sit next to the guy everyone thinks is strange and be his friend.

Pay that widow's utility bill.

Obedience isn't a ball and chain. Rather, it's liberty in Christ. It's the most freeing feeling possible. It is life itself.

We are stewards of all of Christ's resources, especially our hearts. The overflow of an abiding disciple of Christ is natural, not forced. I'm convinced from God's Word and from experience that the thriving Christian will give of the financial, physical, and spiritual resources with which God has entrusted him.

I could write about financial stewardship, teaching Sunday school, entering the mission field, loving on orphans and widows, and any number of other ways to reach out. But in our workaday worlds, in the drudgery of life, what matters is how our lives and tongues confess Jesus to the people in the places where he has planted us. Our thriving in Christ surfaces when we share our faith, disciple others, and carry out acts of love and compassion.

We easily concede that glorifying God is our mission. Yet I've seen a lot of followers of Jesus who rarely want to admit that reaching out to others is the method God has chosen for us to accomplish the mission.

Point to Remember

*The thriving believer does what
God says to reach out to others.*

CHAPTER 19

LENS OF THE GOSPEL

I'm thankful that much of the New Testament was written by the biggest sinner the world has ever known.

At least that's what the apostle Paul considered himself to be.

In 1 Timothy 1:12–16, Paul pauses to offer a glimpse of what he was like before his radical conversion. He tells his young protégé, Timothy, that the Lord has used him in spite of his ugly record. He admits that he once was a blasphemer of God, a persecutor of Christians, and an insolent opponent of the Savior he now serves. Then in verse 15 he drops a statement that has become well-known: "The saying is trustworthy and deserving of full acceptance, that Christ Jesus came into the world to save sinners, of whom I am the foremost."

Paul claims he's the worst sinner who ever lived. While it is an example of his humility, I love how he put a special emphasis on his claim. He introduces the sentence by saying, "This next statement is true and should be believed by all." In other words, one of the only times in his letters when Paul gets in our grill and says "you really need to hear what I'm saying" is to tell us he's a dork.

It's pretty awesome that a guy who was elevated so high in spiritual matters was still keeping his humble place at the feet of Jesus.

Why did Paul see himself in such a radical way? Because Christ had changed him, and he was able to look at where he came from and where he was going through the lens of the gospel. Paul had been one of the religious elite, among the most highly regarded people in society. Yet through surrender and obedience to Christ, Paul's vision had changed to the point that he considered everything outside of knowing Jesus to be rubbish (Philippians 3:8). To see with Christ's eyes is to have an eternal perspective, which is essential for us in our reaching out. If we are to know God and make him known, it matters how we see God and how we see ourselves.

Is Christ the center of your life, or are you the center of your life?

I often tell the story of one of our students who joined our youth group for a day at Islands of Adventure Theme Park at Universal Studios in Orlando, Florida. He sat right behind me as I accompanied several of our kids on the Spiderman roller coaster. The ride requires 3-D glasses.

Shortly after the ride began, the kid started his critique. "This is dumb," he said. A few seconds later, he blurted out, "This is stupid." It took all the restraint I could muster not to turn around halfway through the ride and tell him to zip it.

As soon as we got off the roller coaster, I turned to give him a stern look of disapproval, but any inclination to chastise him faded when I realized why he had been so outspoken. He wasn't wearing his glasses.

The kid had endured the ride with a hazy, blurred lack of focus that would've cleared if only he had worn his 3-D glasses. He couldn't enjoy all that the ride had for him because he couldn't see with the clarity that the makers of the ride had intended. The Bible says that out of the overflow of the heart the mouth speaks (Luke 6:45). In the same way, the condition of our heart determines what our eyes see. The more we follow God and obey him, the less we are conformed to this world and the more our minds are renewed. The more our minds are renewed, the more we are conformed to the image of Christ and see with his eyes.

When our perspective is temporal and our focus is on this life, we will not reach out to others. We will reach in to ourselves. When God made "you shall have no other gods before me" the first of his Ten Commandments (Exodus 20:3), he knew our biggest temptation would be to make gods of ourselves. When we sit on the throne of our lives instead of giving God his rightful place, we can't see past ourselves, much less see other people the way he sees them.

However, when we soak our minds and hearts with God's Word, when we follow the Holy Spirit's prompts to pray for others and act on their behalf, our vision changes. We see with the compassion and clarity of Christ.

I've had to learn my own lessons about seeing the way Jesus wants me to see. A lot of times, youth pastors dream of the perfect student leader—the kid who would change the local high school if he or she would just surrender to the Lord and live out loud for him. Scripture doesn't make such promises, but somewhere in our heads we think if we got that tall, handsome, awesome, up-front football player or cheerleader, and if that kid could just get it together, this town would change. But a lot of us are focused on the quarterback when it's the water boy who is going to change the world.

I have to catch myself whenever I'm tempted to overlook people whom God wants to use for his glory.

I recently studied the Old Testament book of Ruth. It tells the story of Ruth and Naomi, Ruth's mother-in-law. Naomi loses her husband and sons, thereby leaving her in a strange land with strange people and only her two daughters-in-law, including Ruth, as family. In the end, Ruth demonstrates amazing faithfulness to her mother-in-law, staying with her even when Naomi returned to her native Bethlehem, a strange land with a people strange to Ruth herself. Naomi originally urged Ruth to go back home. But Naomi also showed great patience and love after Ruth declined, allowing Ruth to live with her without speaking another word of protest.

The lesson I walked away with was that you can't pick your Timothys (or your Ruths). Sometimes God picks them for you. And they're not people about whom you would normally think, "These are the ones I'm going to attach my life to and pour into." In a way, Naomi got stuck with Ruth and felt compelled to allow her to live with her in Bethlehem. Naomi didn't ask for Ruth, a Moabite woman whom Naomi's son had married. When Naomi's son died, it left Naomi with her daughter-in-law. So she was like, "Oh. Well, I guess it's us."

If we're not sensitive to how the Lord wants us to see people, sometimes we'll miss the friendships God has for us that would've been awesome. Sometimes we'll miss relationships because we can't see the connection. We've already figured out what our best friends are supposed to look like. They're supposed to have the exact same interests as us and laugh at all our jokes. They like honey mustard sauce, just like we do. We try to pick our best friends based on things we have in common, but true best friends often don't have that much in common. They just click.

I've made the mistake of prejudging people plenty of times. I've banked everything on the quarterback and didn't even notice that this other kid in the youth group is the one who is loving on everybody and praying for everybody and seeking God. I saw the light a few years ago. Now, when you watch my ministry, I don't have a cool crowd. I don't gravitate to a particular group. I don't hang with just the band or just the jocks. I hang with whoever comes to me and wants to go share the love of Jesus with others, and we go together. God has shown me that I shortchange what he wants to do when I don't see the world the way he sees it.

How well do you see? Do you have your God-glasses on? It's up to us to sharpen the focus through spiritual disciplines and obedience, but Jesus always gives his followers a new way to see things.

Even our past, present, and future.

Point to Remember

Jesus gives us a new way to see the world.

CHAPTER 20

SCARS

Like most people, I have scars on different parts of my body. My scars send a message. They say that I exist and that I'm here to be a warning for others. Don't do what I just did.

Have you ever stopped someone from trying a stunt by pointing to a scar and saying, "Wait! Let me show you what happens when you do that"?

Scars come with benefits. Scars can make you smarter. Every time I grab a box cutter, I have one thought: *Lord in heaven, please do not let me do* that *again!*

I've taught people to be careful with knives my whole life, but while using a box cutter for a weekend event, I cut in the wrong direction and sliced a chunk out of my thumb. Several stitches later, I had a scar on the way. For the next several years, when we passed out box cutters to prepare for an event, guess who did not pick up one. I found a way to work on posters.

Scars can serve as a warning to be more cautious. But other kinds of scars just haunt us. They stay with us and change everything about us. They can even change what we decide we believe about God.

Many people have been Christians for years, maybe even for most of their lives, and trudge through a defeated life thinking, *Some of my biggest failures have been since I was saved.* How are we supposed to deal with that?

Think back to Paul's life. He began as an enemy of the church. Jesus changed him as he headed to Damascus to put more Christians in jail. He intended to tear apart more families and maybe even kill more people. He had watched the stoning of the first Christian martyr, Stephen. Then Jesus stopped Paul in his tracks and changed his heart. Think he had some scars in his life?

There's no verse for this, but I wonder if Paul ever went into a city to spread the gospel and stood to preach before someone whose parents were in prison at that moment because of him.

The thing about scars is, they don't go away.

Believers sometimes send mixed messages. We say, "Stay away from sin. You have to run from this junk because it's going to mess you up." Then we toss in the confusing part: "But if you do mess up, God will totally forgive you and restore you."

Both messages are true, but they prompt legitimate

questions I hear all the time. For example, someone might tell me, "You know, I hear Christians saying I need to stay away from sin. But for everyone who has already blown it, they say, 'It's all good. God takes care of it.' Why not just do what I told my parents when I was a teenager — 'I need to make my own mistakes'?"

It leaves us thinking maybe it's not that big a deal to fail. But *is* it a big deal?

Yes.

As bad and ugly and disfiguring as physical scars are, spiritual scars cut much deeper and haunt us much longer. Any time we step forward to follow Jesus, what does the Accuser do? He points to our scars. *Remember that time you stood up in front of everyone and made your profession of faith and said, "I'm all for Jesus now"? How did that go? Or how about that time you signed your little purity commitment when you were a teenager? How did that turn out for you?*

The Enemy constantly points to our failures. So how should we answer him? The same way Jesus did. With Scripture. Here's an example:

Paul knew we all have scars, but he tells us that's not a negative. Paul sees his past as his past. One verse after saying he is the worst sinner ever, he offers us this hope: "I received mercy for this reason, that in me, as the foremost, Jesus Christ might display his perfect patience" (1 Timothy 1:16).

Philippians shows that Paul dealt with his scars in a clever way. He *used them* to trumpet God's grace both to himself concerning his past and to others concerning their future.

In Philippians 3, Paul counters false teachers who boast about themselves. He recites a long list of reasons that he could boast about himself if he wanted, but then he does something unexpected. He says he counts every bit of his accomplishments as rubbish compared to the surpassing worth of knowing Jesus and making him known.

Paul says his new goal is to be found in Christ with a righteousness not his own but with one that comes through faith in Jesus. Then comes Philippians 3:12–14:

Not that I have already obtained this or am already perfect, but I press on to make it my own, because Christ Jesus has made me his own. Brothers, I do not consider that I have made it my own. But one thing I do: forgetting what lies behind and straining forward to what lies ahead, I press on toward the goal for the prize of the upward call of God in Christ Jesus.

In other words, Paul tells his friends in Philippi, "I'm not done yet. I'm like half-baked cornbread. If you look inside of me spiritually, it's just a giant vat of mush that's not complete." Paul says he presses on but he's not spiritually perfected. But one thing he does—he forgets about his past. Not that he doesn't remember those events. They're impossible to forget. He just reckons himself righteous because Jesus said he is, and he chooses not to allow those past mistakes to dictate his present and future. He presses on toward the goals that God has for his life, which are to grow closer to Jesus and to tell others about him.

In the previous chapter, I showed you 1 Timothy 1:15. It's

one of those verses where Paul rolls up his sleeves and lets us all in on his scars. He admits he blasphemed God and persecuted followers of Christ. He admits he was an "insolent opponent" of Jesus (verse 13). I also showed you verse 16, but I intentionally edited out the verse's final phrase. "I received mercy for this reason, that in me, as the foremost, Jesus Christ might display his perfect patience *as an example to those who were to believe in him for eternal life*" (emphasis added).

Paul talked about his scars to give an example to those with whom he shared the gospel. He realized he had to keep it real.

I talked about scars in a church service one night and asked people to share the stories behind their scars. Hands went up all over the room. Arms, ankles, knees, elbows, and eyebrows brought giggles as cameras highlighted their scars on the big screen. But if I had waited until the end of the message and said, "Show us your real scars. Share your failures and how you have blown it," a hush would have fallen over the room.

Something weird happens when church people get together. We feel we need to live to honor God, but we can never let others see our weaknesses. We can never be less than our spiritual best. That's when you get the folks who spit out, "Hey, brother. God's good, ain't he? Bless God, I'm better than I deserve."

A lot of us pretend everything is OK when it's really not. We think the platform holding the pulpit and choir loft is the only stage in the room, but it's not. The biggest stage is out in the crowd. More performances happen in the congregation than anywhere else. We're cut up and beat up, and we're scared to let anybody know it because we have to look like we have it all together. There's just not a verse for that either.

Church is the place to be broken together. It's the place to say, "I really need y'all to pray for me because I'm not in the Word and I'm not praying and I don't really want to do either one. Pray for me."

We all want a safe haven, but we have to be willing to be transparent ourselves. Most of the time, we blame everyone else and start church shopping. I can't tell you how many times I've heard, "I want to find a place where I can be myself." What this person means is, "I want to find some people who are real." Instead, wouldn't it honor God if *we all* sought to be real?

If you're hurting and think you're failing, you have to talk to somebody. I sit with teenagers almost every day who finally are breaking down and being transparent. They don't parrot Christianese and claim that they've been perfect in their quiet time. At long last, they're saying, "I'm stinking this up and I don't know why, and I hate myself for it."

God can handle your scars. So can any genuine, loving Christian. There always will be somebody who raises an eyebrow at what you say, but you still need to open up to the body of Christ around you and start being the person you wish everybody else would be. Don't worry about being judged by people. It's far worse to never change and ultimately face God's judgment. We all have to start being honest with God and honest with each other.

It has to start with someone saying, "I have scars, and I'm

afraid God doesn't love me anymore. I need to know what to do."

I have to use the eyes of Jesus when I look at my past. I have to accept that his Word says my past is paid for and my slate is wiped clean. Jesus took my sin and spread it as far as the east is from the west. It's gone.

But ...

But I can't act like it didn't happen. Instead of my past haunting me and dragging me back into it, I can use it. If I see my past through the eyes of Jesus, then I see it as fodder for another soul. I see it as my story that I can use to build a bridge to someone else (more on this in chapter 28).

Your scars are your road map to God's grace in your life.

If we act like we have it all together, not only is it untrue but everyone sees through the façade as well. Phony never led anyone to Jesus. If we would see some of the bad choices we've made as a way to point other people to Jesus, we would allow Jesus to go Romans 8:28 on our past and turn it into good. Some people believe their past is so bad that not even God can redeem it, but God said he makes *all things* new (Revelation 21:5).

With Jesus guiding your words, one of the most powerful spiritual statements you could ever make goes something like this: "If God can save me, he can save anybody. Let me run down my résumé with you real quick. Let me tell you where I've been." *That* is the power of transparency.

When you seek to thrive by digging deep to grow your roots, God explains who he is and who you are, and you see your past in a different light. It doesn't scare you anymore. You don't worry about people discovering your skeletons. You don't freak out about your weaknesses anymore because you see that the Bible is full of fools, outlaws, and ordinary people. God used them, and his Word will convince you that he'll use you too.

Some of us don't think we can get past our past. We don't have to. God took care of our past and is ready to hand it back to us, redeemed, as his tool.

Thankfully, that tool is not a box cutter.

Point to Remember

We can use our scars as a road map of God's grace in our lives.

CHAPTER 21

NEXT THING

The people against whom Jesus railed in righteous indignation were the ones who practiced religion. His harshest condemnation fell on the Pharisees and Sadducees, the religious elite of the day. He knew they banked everything on how they were perceived by others.

Many of us good Christians crave the approval of others too, but we would call the Pharisees ridiculous. We would say, "You can't be good enough to reach God. It's stupid to even conceive of such a notion. We're all train wrecks before a holy God."

But how many of us have at least had this thought: *Man, I've gone too far for God to reach me now!* It's the reverse sentiment the Pharisees had, but it leaves us just as skeptical of

God's grace. The Pharisees thought their goodness could get them to God, and we think our badness can chase him off.

Jesus constantly battles the lies bouncing around in our heads. One of them is our security in Christ—how we see our future. This is an important point because if you believe you're a child of God forever, you'll live a life of gratitude and freedom and act like a child of God forever.

The Pharisees said, "Abraham was our great-great-great-great-great-grandfather. So we're in. We're safe."

It's like one of us saying, "I go to XYZ Church, just like my family did before me. So I'm saved. I'm going to heaven."

In both cases, Jesus has one answer. "Before Abraham was, I am" (John 8:58).

You couldn't pass an English exam with that grammar. Only one person can use this sentence and not get a big, red X on his paper.

Jesus made that statement during one of his most heated exchanges with Jewish leaders. It was an explicit claim to deity. They knew exactly what he meant, and they picked up stones to try to kill him. The truth is in the tense Jesus uses.

He's saying that back before creation, back before the world was a ball, he am. At the end of all of this, when this world is over and all of your goals and dreams and pursuits are done, when your great-great-great-great-great-grandkids' dreams are over, when space and time are transformed and this place is back to being nothing ... he am.

Jesus is no "I was." He's no "I will be."

Jesus *am*.

Nobody else can say that. No one else can say that time doesn't confine him and that he is ever present. Go walk around the mall today and blurt out "I am" a few times and see what kind of looks you get. The security guard on the Segway will escort you straight to the exit. Or have a straitjacket waiting for you.

So many of us obsess over our lives. We fret over our past because we're afraid it will either come back to bite us or we'll fall back into it. At the same time, we sweat our future because we don't want to end up like "they" did (whoever "they" are to whom we compare ourselves).

We act as if we must solve a giant riddle, and we'll be toast if we don't solve it just right. Sometimes we try to numb ourselves to the thought. It's like turning up the music in our cars so we can't hear the noises our dying engines are making. Maybe they won't break down if we don't hear them.

We pray and beg for God to show us his will as if we're spiritual paupers. God is not a cosmic Santa Claus who has loaded the Christmas tree of his will with a hundred wrapped boxes with no names on them. He isn't standing back and laughing at us as we try to figure out which one is meant for our lives. If we are digging into God's Word and reaching out to his world, then we *are* his will.

Either we believe God is sovereign and arranges all of our circumstances, or we believe some things are beyond his control. If we believe the latter, that means we believe in whim and happenstance. That means we believe in chaos. That means we believe things happen *to* God.

I often talk to young people who are scared to death that they're going to marry the wrong person. They've been burned by the divorce of someone close to them. They either suffered personally or saw it up close, and they're petrified of failing in marriage.

I have one answer for them: "Do you know that right now God is in heaven and sees you sitting on your front porch and watching your grandkids play? You know why? Because he am."

Another time I might say, "Do you realize you're mortified over college, and yet God is watching you walk across the stage to accept your degree right now? Because he am. He's already there."

We're all guilty of living in anticipation of a fork in the road. There is no fork in your road. God didn't ask you to make any huge decisions. All he said was, "Lean on me, see like I see, and realize your past is gone and your future is mine. All I ask is that you get to know me and make me known."

God hasn't called us to something in a year. We're called for the here and now. We were not made to survive today for some potential future endeavor, something that maybe he'll do through us one day.

We're looking so forward to tomorrow that we're tripping over today. Then when we get to tomorrow, we start worrying about the next tomorrow. Everything counts, especially today.

God has placed you where you are totally on purpose. Don't spoil it by anticipating or dreading your future. God didn't call you to figure out what happens next. He's already there. He's at the end of your life looking back on it right now. He wants you to rest in that truth, rest in who he made you to be, and dig your roots in and know him.

The more you know him, the more his truth clarifies all your relationships and decisions.

The more you know him, you realize things like, *I don't think I need do that again this year. I'm supposed to do this over here for now.*

The more you know him, the more you realize, *I need to talk to that guy over there because nobody is really talking to him anymore.*

If Jesus is in you, then I encourage you to make a decision of your will and say to him, "Thank you, God, for making me who I am. Thank you for forgiving me of my past and teaching me lessons from it. I'm going to follow your lead from here on out."

You just told him you appreciate your past, present, and future. You also just saw them the way he does.

Doing big things for God is not some grand movement to shoot for in the future. Doing big things for God just means doing the very next thing he says. It's the very next person you need to love on and forgive. It's the very next person to tell about Jesus. It's the very next temptation to resist. One decision at a time, we seek to look at it the way Jesus does and trust him for the results.

Are you *surviving* life right now, or are you *thriving* inside of life right now? Survivors tend to think that tomorrow will be easier; tomorrow will work out better; and if I can just get to tomorrow, I'm going to be OK.

We'll always anticipate another tomorrow, and tomorrow will never fill us. Only I Am will bring us fulfillment and peace now.

God wants you to see with the eyes of Jesus right here and now in your present. Keep your eyes open. What we tend to see as road cones on life's highway are really people God brings into our path.

If Jesus stood bodily before me right now, I believe he'd tell me to take a deep breath, look into his eyes, and listen closely. He'd say to me, "If you would just dig in to me and sink in to who I've made you and see people like I see them, when you get to the end of the week, you wouldn't think, *Finally. I'm free of this place for a while.* Instead, you'd say, *I hope I made a difference in someone's life this week, and I can't wait to get started again.*"

The way we see determines our outlook for each new day. If I see with Jesus' eyes in the present, I'll see a purpose for being where he has me right now. He tells us to redeem the time, and the time is now.

Because he am.

Point to Remember

God doesn't want us to live in the future but in his Now.

CHAPTER 22

APPOINTMENTS

Have you ever noticed that the disciples get a bad rap all throughout the four Gospels? They mess up a lot. Jesus corrects them a lot. Then they mess up again.

For one, Jesus didn't like how they viewed other people. The disciples seemed to be bothered by anyone not in their group. When the crowds pressed in, they tried to shoo them away. When the crowds were hungry, they tried to send them home. And when little children ran up to Jesus, the disciples shook their heads. "Lord, do you want us to get these kids out of here?"

It's as though the disciples wanted to be with Jesus and wanted to be a part of big things, but the idea of laying down their lives for strangers appeared foreign.

Ministry is great until people show up. We can be fired up about doing really cool spiritual things, and then when people get in front of us, life gets hard. They don't listen. They have their own ideas. It's easy to shy away and decide, *I just prefer to be a very deep believer.* If all we do is suck in knowledge, we'll find that it puffs up. On the other hand, love builds up.

Matthew 9:35–38 describes a typical scene in Jesus' earthly ministry:

> And Jesus went throughout all the cities and villages, teaching in their synagogues and proclaiming the gospel of the kingdom and healing every disease and every affliction. When he saw the crowds, he had compassion for them, because they were harassed and helpless, like sheep without a shepherd. Then he said to his disciples, "The harvest is plentiful, but the laborers are few; therefore pray earnestly to the Lord of the harvest to send out laborers into his harvest."

One particular word stands out in the middle of this story. It's only three letters long: s-a-w. "When he *saw* the crowds, he had compassion on them."

Sure, the images of these people registered on the retinas of the disciples. But they did not *see* these people. Jesus did.

There is something about the way Jesus sees people that causes me to want to know him more.

Until we have a true love for Jesus, until we search out his heart, our hearts will not be broken by what breaks his. The more I walk with God—not practicing religion or doing ministry but getting to know the person of Jesus — the more I see people the way he sees them. When I start seeing people like he sees them, I start hurting like he does.

Even better, when I spend time with him and I'm grounded in his Word, I minister out of pure motives and not sappy emotionalism. Sappy emotionalism runs out of steam. Biblically grounded and Spirit-led outreach, in contrast, stays consistent and strong, like the thick branches of a giant oak.

When you walk into your office or your school, do *you* see people as road cones on your way to bigger and better things? Or do you see them as God's providential appointments to reach for him? Sometimes we want to pick the crowd for our ministry efforts. We want a crowd that thinks we're awesome or that respects us and listens to everything we say. But God has put us where we are for his reasons.

Guess where Jesus is ministering in Matthew 9? His home base. It is his home folk, the people in Galilee who know him best. He knows their spiritual condition. Better than anyone else, he knows they're wretches full of wickedness. Yet when he sees them, he has compassion on them. That pricks my heart.

Here is what I want to pray for myself and what I challenge you to pray: *Lord, help me to see the people you've placed around me like you see them.*

When we see people the way God sees them, our attitude changes. That guy who is obnoxious and always barks about something? Maybe he's the most insecure person in the office and needs encouragement. The girl who seems to be consumed with finding another guy? Maybe she doesn't have a dad. Maybe if we were a little closer to our own heavenly Father, we could see with his eyes.

When I read the Matthew 9 passage, I imagine Jesus pushing his way through the crowds and reaching out to touch everyone he passes. A teenage girl whose arm is curled up—he reaches over and touches her, and her arm straightens out. He opens a deaf guy's ears. He heals a blind woman. A little girl who couldn't talk is suddenly yelling and laughing with her parents. I can just imagine Jesus turning around and looking at his disciples as if to say, "Do you see what I see?"

"The harvest is plentiful, but the laborers are few; therefore pray earnestly to the Lord of the harvest to send out laborers into his harvest." The irony is that this passage concludes Matthew 9. In the very next chapter, right before the first verse, my Bible includes a subtitle that reads, "Jesus Sends Out the Twelve." What's happening? "All right, boys," Jesus says. "Pair up. We're going out." So one chapter closes with Jesus urging prayer for more laborers for the gospel, and the next chapter opens with Jesus doing something about it. Guess who he used? The people closest to him.

When we ask God to do something—save our unbelieving friend or send someone to witness to our boss—we'd better be ready. He will turn around that prayer and place his calling on us. We're going to be the answer to our own prayer.

May we understand that the place God has put us and the people around us are the harvest field. We're the laborers in the harvest field. He's given us everything we need to share. He's given us a story, scars and all, and he's given us his eyes, his Spirit, and his Word. We're ready. All that remains is to love somebody like Jesus does.

Point to Remember

*Seeing people as Jesus sees them spurs us
to treat them as he does.*

CHAPTER 23

THE X FACTOR

Remember the lesson of the eagle and the yardbird in chapter 5?

People often tell me they feel like they're supposed to be doing something for the Lord. They don't know the churchy words for it, but what they describe is a growing realization that God has a different idea for their life than they do. They're not sure what to do with this inner tug. They start getting all Iggy with it. They know they're designed for something else. They see something missing, and then God shows them that they're the missing piece.

When you give Jesus your life, the Holy Spirit moves in. The Spirit brings talents, insights, and understanding that you didn't possess before. Those gifts are like glasses with different colored lenses for you to see the world. You see life through your personality, experiences, and gifts.

I once heard Pastor Tony Evans say that the area of the church about which you find yourself most critical is probably the area where you're supposed to serve. You're seeing a hole that only you can see—because that's your gift. You see the impersonal aspect of your church because your gift is hospitality. You see the widows who need assistance because your gift is mercy. You see the flaws in the small group leader's lesson because your gift is teaching.

This is one way God shows us where we might need to serve. When we don't respond, we often turn bitter. Often, the most critical people are the ones who never stepped up and used their gifts.

Another consistent statement I hear is "I need to be in ministry, but I'm just not good in front of people." When someone says this to me, it tells me that he or she believes ministry is confined to singing and talking on a stage.

Unfortunately, we've all learned this perspective from the personality-centric church. We've figured out that ministry is performed by people raised on a platform two or three feet above the rest of us, and we all go and watch them on Sunday.

When you don't see yourself standing in front of people, you think, *I guess ministry is not for me, because I can't fit into any of the public roles.*

That's just not in the Bible.

God says that whatever you do in word or deed, do it all

for the glory of the Lord. When you work, work as though working for the Lord. Use your gifts. Pour into the body. Christ is the head, but you're an arm or a leg or some other part. You are needed to make the body function.

You may also have the idea that God is preparing you for some great endeavor in the future. And he may well be preparing you for something. But when you're called to something, you're called now. If you feel like your ministry is to pour into people, you need to ask God how to do it now. God is not calling you to something in a year. He's calling you to something now.

Furthermore, when you sense God's call, be hesitant to stick it in a box and decide what it is on your own.

During summer camp of 2013, we had about 30 students out of 240 decide that God was calling them to some sort of missions work. The first thing I told these 30 was to be cool with what they already knew. "Don't feel like you need to know more than you do right now or have a title on it or have a country picked out just because you think God has called you," I said. "Hold out your hand with your palm up. God just dropped a little something in your hand, and your job is to not clench your fist and run with it and do as you please. Keep holding open your hand and let God add or take away as he pleases. Let him have his way. It all came from him anyway."

I learned that lesson the hard way. I thought God was calling me to music ministry because I could sing. I grabbed hold of the talent I knew I had, put it in a box, and took off. And I almost missed student ministry. It wasn't until I was in college, pursuing a music major, that I stumbled upon using my gifts in student ministry. When a church asked me to lead their youth, it caught me off-guard. But I sensed God's call even as I continued my studies. I obeyed that call, and that obedience has shaped my life. In serving the Lord, I'm a student pastor before I'm a singer, songwriter, and worship leader.

Jake and Jesse are two high school seniors in our ministry. Jesse thinks he's called to something in the church, maybe leading worship through music. Jake is an honor graduate who believes he's called to ministry but also feels he needs to be a doctor.

We started praying through it, and I clarified something. "Guys, I'm not getting extra preacher points for making more preachers," I said. "You need to do whatever God has created you to do and make disciples there."

Roger Glidewell of Global Youth Ministries often teaches at our summer camps. He told our kids the story of Moses and the burning bush (Exodus 3–4).

"Any old bush would do," he said. "Why was it a bush? Why wasn't it a tree? When something is on fire and not burning up, it doesn't really matter what it is."

It hit me that the bush was still just being a bush. It didn't have anything extra in it. There wasn't an extra chemical. It was just a bush and nothing more, and it brought all it had to the table. The fire was not from the bush.

All David had was his sling and his rocks. He brought them to the table and God used him.

God will use whatever you bring to the table, but he also will add something only he can add. We limit God because we can't figure out the X factor—the ingredient he adds. All we see is what we can do, and we think that's too insignificant.

But God says, "Hey, any old bush will do here. You just be ready, because if you follow me, I'm going to throw in the fire. That's nowhere in your backpack. Nowhere."

Moses had a long list of excuses. He had emotional, physical, and spiritual reasons why he couldn't obey God's command to return to Egypt and deliver the Israelites from bondage. He had painted his own picture of the person God uses. In his excuses, he described the man he thought God *should* use.

It's like he went up to a whiteboard and started drawing a stick figure to point out all his shortcomings. "I don't speak well. I don't know enough about you, God. Who do I tell them you are? They won't listen to me. I'm not enough. I'm not smart enough. I'm not talented enough."

When he made all these excuses, he sketched the person he thought God was supposed to use. In so many words, God answered, "You have to let me erase your goofy picture of perfection."

When God called me to ministry, I considered my dyslexia a hindrance. I didn't see what I had to offer even on my best day. The real hindrance was my refusal to consider the X factor of God's intervention.

You're here on purpose, weaknesses included. You are all God's fault.

God doesn't call extroverted people to be introverted or introverted people to be extroverted. He doesn't call creative people to handle the church calendar, and he doesn't call detailed people to write dramas. He made you totally on purpose.

The Bible shows that God used both Dr. Luke and John the Baptist. Those guys probably never would have hung out together. You've got one guy sitting there munching on a bug right next to a doctor with sterile flatware. Ain't gonna happen.

God also knits together your personality for whatever he's called you to do. Does your personality need work? Yes, it will need work for the rest of your life. This isn't one of those areas where you can say, "This is just the way I am." That statement never follows a positive event, as in "I led this person to Jesus because this is just who I am." No, it's always, "I just lost my temper because this is just who I am." Or, "I just blistered this person in front of everybody because I'm honest to a fault. That's just who I am."

God uses his Holy Spirit to work the *you* part out of you. He always works on your rough edges, but God doesn't want you to be somebody you're not. God can use you just where you are—your gifts, talents, and strengths—but in using you, he will change you and conform you to look more like Christ.

Listen to that inner tug. See the hole you're supposed to fill. Get to work on your calling now rather than later. Learn the lessons God sends to mold you. Most of all, expect the X factor. Expect God to send the fire.

In 1 Corinthians 2, the apostle Paul in effect says, "When I came to you, I didn't come with lofty speech and wisdom, but I came with a demonstration of God's power. I didn't want to rob the cross of its power by getting in the way. I decided to know nothing among you except Jesus Christ." Paul *decided* this not because he didn't have talent. God equipped him with knowledge, skills, writing ability, and oratory talent. But Paul realized this truth: As much as God will take us as we are, we have to understand that on our best day — when our talents and skills are at their peak and we're in the best mood we've ever experienced — absolutely nothing supernatural will happen. If God doesn't step in, the moment will carry no eternal weight. At our best, all we can ever really be is available.

Like any old bush.

Point to Remember

God will use us right where we are to thrive.

CHAPTER 24

ORNAMENTS

The fruit of the Spirit, as listed in Galatians 5:22–23, is love, joy, peace, patience, kindness, goodness, faithfulness, gentleness, and self-control.

Notice that the Bible does not call these attributes the "fruits of the Spirit" (plural). Taken together, they're the "fruit of the Spirit" (singular), meaning that where the Spirit of God is present, all of these attributes are present in some degree. Some are present more than others, but they're all there.

We also forget that we cannot hang fruit. We try to hang it, but the graft fails every time. Our errant picture of who God is and who we are often goes something like this: *Now that he's shown us awesomeness, we should go be awesome.* And we stink at it.

Well, that verse says we've got to be patient, so I'm going to go try some patience today. Right.

I've tried this self-dependent approach before, and God crashed my personal party with a clear message: "If you'll dig your roots down deep in me, I'll produce the fruit. Just know me and learn who you are in me. Now that you know who I am and that I'm in control and that I'm bigger than your past and stronger than your weakness and can reach further than you can run, and now that you know that you're new and your old is gone, and you're not trying to stay saved but I've got you—*now* go do life. As you're doing life, I'm going to give you a chance to be patient today. Don't create moments. It's going to happen."

You can't hang fruit. The fruit of the Spirit is the fruit of the *Spirit*. It's not the fruit of Mark or the fruit of [insert your name].

It's also easy to fall into the trap of thinking, *The fruit proves the tree is alive, and if there's no fruit, I'm not even saved. I'm going to get cut down and burned.* The Enemy works to make us think we must produce fruit to prove to God—and to ourselves—that we belong to him. This is where we fall into the tailspin of thinking that what we do determines who we are. We believe quotes like "what a man does defines him." Those great sayings sound like they come from a Batman movie. But your efforts can't define you to God.

So what does define a follower of Jesus?

Whatever you thought first in answer to this question is your definition of a Christian. Does it match Scripture? If what just popped into your head involves anything you *do*, you're in trouble. What if you don't do that tomorrow? Or the next day?

This thinking bogs you down in fear. You never know the cutoff date. How long can you not do it before you're not in? No one will call and tell you. You must come up with something yourself, and a lot of churches have done so. They create their own requirements to determine who's in and who's not. Most of the time, those requirements don't square with God's Word.

The fruit of the Spirit is produced when we instinctively seek out nourishment. My previous album and book were all about Jesus being *The Well*, the source of living water for believers. Our job is simply to know him, to be fed and refreshed by him, to thrive in him, to rest in him, and to love him. Paul said his goal was to "be found in him, not having a righteousness of my own that comes from the law, but that which comes through faith in Christ, the righteousness from God that depends on faith — that I may know him and the power of his resurrection" (Philippians 3:9–10).

If you were to place a real apple beside one of those fake apples that collect dust in a kitchen table bowl, you could tell the difference at a glance. God sees that kind of difference when you try to work your way to him versus allowing him to work his way out of you.

Paul tells us in Philippians 2:12 to work out our own salvation with fear and trembling. We've taken that one verse and isolated it in the back of our heads as we wrangle through the faith-versus-works battle. But the next verse reads, "For it is God who works in you, both to will and to work for his good pleasure."

He's worked his life into you, and now you have to work it out. It's not a salvation question, because he's already in you. He's in you in the person of his Holy Spirit, and that is a fact. It's done. In the process of growing you, God tries to work himself into all of your life and into how you react to people and circumstances.

For me, God has to work in me to control my smart mouth. If I'm wronged or on the bad end of a sarcastic comment or joke, my first thought is usually not nice. I go through a list of responses in my head and hope I don't say a bad one. I haven't allowed God to have all of me in that area yet. He's still working himself in, and my first instinct is still to say the smart-mouth thing.

In the June 6 devotional of his classic book *My Utmost for His Highest*, Oswald Chambers writes this:

> With focused attention and great care, you have to "work out" what God "works in" you — not *work* to accomplish or earn "your own salvation," but *work it out* so you will exhibit the evidence of a life based with determined, unshakable faith on the complete and perfect redemption of the Lord. As you do this, you do not bring an opposing will up against God's will — God's will *is* your will. Your natural choices will be in accordance with God's will, and living this life will be as natural as breathing.[*]

---

* Oswald Chambers, *My Utmost for His Highest* (Grand Rapids: Discovery House, 2006), June 6.

That's our fight now—working it out, allowing the Holy Spirit to mold us and produce fruit through us.

Lately, I've been telling a lot of my students who are high school seniors one simple message: "For a long time, your life has been Wednesday night Thrive services, DNow weekends, Breakout summer camp, and Thrive University on Sunday nights. It's all little logos and fill-in-the-blank worksheets and follow-the-leader worship services with certain songs. But now you're about to walk out into a hostile world, and the training wheels are off. Now your faith is trying to fight its way out of your quiet time and into your life. God is in you and encouraging you that he and your faith really and truly were in you all along. And he says, 'Now let me start doing life through you and help you make choices.'"

I've started asking myself questions lately.

Am I giving to be blessed? Or am I blessed, so I'm giving?

Am I serving to be loved? Or am I loved, so I'm serving?

Matthew 5–6 prompted these questions about my good deeds and whether I do them to be seen, heard, loved, or respected. Jesus says, "If those are your motives, well, congratulations. You have your reward." Those are ornaments. He called the Pharisees whitewashed tombs for all their pretty ornaments.

Fake fruit are plastic and hollow. They're pretty and shiny ornaments, but they nourish no one. Many people have bitten into ornaments piously offered in the name of Christ, and that's why they don't come to church. They've chomped down on plastic fruit—from their parents and from other

Christians who were a mile wide and an inch deep—and they're still as empty as the ornaments they tried.

Jesus has an answer. "Just know me and make me known. Take the moments I give you. Make the most of every conversation, and let each be seasoned with salt. Look for me and chase after me. In whatever opportunities I send your way, whatever is the very next thing I say to do, do it with all your heart."

That is God's will for your life.

Point to Remember

We can't produce the fruit of the Spirit; we must yield to God.

CHAPTER 25

THE DOOR

I stopped using Facebook not long ago. I decided I'd read enough "Bless God" comments.

"Bless God, if I have one more day like today, I'm going to tell off my boss."

"Bless God, I've about had enough of her junk."

And this was from fellow believers.

Facebook is scary. My own posts weren't too crazy, but the responses to my posts sometimes left me shaking my head. It reminded me that one of the reasons people in the world hear that Christians hate them is because they're actually hearing that Christians hate them.

God's eyes don't see that way. Does he hate the sin? Of

course. Does he love the people he created? Yes, without limit.

Just like parents attempting to have children, God actually tried to have you. He thought about you in advance; he knit you together in your mother's womb; he breathed life into you.

He tried to have all those lost people out there too. Every single one.

Even the atheists.

Even the murderers and rapists.

Even the homosexuals and abortionists.

Not one of them got here without his blessing. He loves them all. The key to thriving with the right perspective is to learn God's Word and yield to his Holy Spirit as you ask him to give you his eyes.

If you look closely, most people's Facebook and Instagram accounts reveal an undercurrent. On the surface, a lot of folks "thank God it's Friday" or count down the days to vacation. They're just surviving until they can have a good time. Underneath it all is a cry. *Is there something more than this?*

When I read Scripture, the tone is different. I don't see anyone in the New Testament talking like that. Instead, they say, "Today is the day I make my stand. Today is the day I live it out."

In my sketch of the giant tree (chapter 2), I wrote "God's Sovereignty" and "Man's Responsibility" in the root system. The sprawling branches that touch the heavens as we reach out have two sides too—"Love" and "Truth."

If we love without the truth, we don't show people an

accurate picture of a holy and just God. If we give people truth without love, we become a clanging cymbal that pushes them away. Just as God's sovereignty and human responsibility are parts of our root system, so truth and love balance our reach.

I wrote earlier that my purpose for this book is to encourage you to thrive. But it is up to you to actually do so. There is no secret to thriving. Nothing is hidden. God spelled it out in his Word, and the only way you'll thrive is if you know his Word and live his Word. If you don't, you won't.

Money and fame do not equate to thriving, nor does a rewarding job. Your job is what you do. If it is who you are, you're in for a miserable ride.

In John 10:10, Jesus says, "The thief comes only to steal and kill and destroy. I came that they may have life and have it abundantly." This is one of the most quoted verses in the Bible. People love it. The prosperity gospel people make tattoos of it. What few people notice is the context. The verse is in the middle of the Good Shepherd passage, where Jesus calls himself first the door of the sheep and then the shepherd of the sheep. He uses analogies to make points. The sheep are symbolic for people, and I challenge you to find a more fitting symbol of people than sheep.

Sheep are stubborn and wayward. They may or may not obey. They are prone to wander. They stink and need constant maintenance. They are susceptible to attacks from thieves and predators.

Satan is the thief in this passage, the one who comes to steal, kill, and destroy. He can't have your soul if you belong to God, but he can steal your joy, kill your hopes, and destroy your dreams. Jesus offers an answer with his next two words in this passage.

"I came."

Jesus came to give us life, and not just mundane life. He came to give us thriving life. But he is the door. He's the way. You have to walk through the door and commit yourself wholeheartedly to him. You can't stand with one foot inside the door and the other foot out in the world and expect to have abundant, thriving life. The thriving life means going all in with Jesus. But going all in with Jesus means being willing to minister how, where, and to whom he wants us to minister. We don't get to pick and choose. It can be scary and even feel uncertain, but it makes for a great adventure, and it thrills the heart of Jesus to no end.

Read the psalms and take note of how often the writer praises the Lord for his mercy (grace) and truth. And John opens his beautiful Gospel with an eyewitness testimony of Jesus and writes, "We have seen his glory, glory as of the only Son from the Father, full of grace and truth" (John 1:14).

The God of the Old Testament is the God of the New Testament, full of grace and truth. If we are to conform to the image of our Savior, then we also will strike the balance between grace and truth. As we will see in the next chapter, then and only then will we convey through reaching others that Jesus is not only our Savior but also a friend of sinners.

Point to Remember

Let's seek to conform to Jesus' balance of grace and truth.

CHAPTER 26

FRIEND OF SINNERS

I wrote a song called "Jesus, Friend of Sinners" for Casting Crowns' album *The Well*. It showed my frustration with the wrong picture of Jesus we believers have given the world. It also vented my feelings about the anger we exhibit toward lost people for sinning. Write down that sentence when you have a moment and read it out loud.

We're angry at lost people for sinning.

We're saved and we're a bunch of train wrecks, but we're mad at the world for doing lost stuff. At least that's the message they're hearing.

If I made that statement as we all sat around a campfire,

most believers would say, "Not true." But it doesn't matter what *we* think. The average lost person makes it clear that we come off otherwise. Now, I realize that some of their reactions come from either conviction or dislike of the truth, but we somehow have to connect with the folks who have the wrong image of God's people and God's love. It's apparent some truth made it out to the world, but love didn't always go with it.

Love earns the right to speak truth. And truth proves that we really love. That's why we have to speak truth in love.

If all you are is truth, you're hammering rules and standards and unreachable goals. If all you are is love, you're giving everything a pass; love wins and everybody is going to be fine. We honor God when we strike a balance between the two.

Instead of being dually minded to include both grace and truth, we often prove we're what James calls double-minded (James 1:8). It goes something like this: When I fail, I pray for mercy. When you fail me, I deliver law. I'm all about grace when I fail. I'm all about law when you fail me.

A simple illustration of the grace-versus-law debate comes when we're behind the wheel of a car. When someone pulls out in front of us, we usually react from our gut. "You idiot. How do you even sit up straight? You have to study and prepare to be as stupid as you are." But when we cut off somebody and she honks at us, our first thought is, *Oh, great. Like you've never made a mistake before.*

How many times have you picked your nose today? But if you look over to another car and see somebody digging in, you think, *Look at that guy. How disgusting!* I don't know why we all think we're invisible when we're sitting in traffic and mining nose gold, but we look just as disgusting to others as they do to us.

My double-minded ways — the way I see me when I fail and the way I see the world when it fails — don't stop with others. I'm also that way with God.

If someone fails me, I want to sit him down and show him charts and graphs. I want him to see that he failed, and I want him to admit that he failed. When I fail? Different story. "Well, God, you know my situation. You know all that stuff from my childhood causes me to think this way."

I maintain an extensive list of excuses. My double-mindedness demands mercy from God while I deal justice to the world. That's why I wrote the lyric "always looking around but never looking up/I'm so double-minded" in "Jesus, Friend of Sinners." I tried to make myself the principal in the song.

It didn't help.

The two main responses I heard about the song are a testament to our struggle with double-mindedness. My heart when I started writing the song is the same heart I have now: *We need to love on people, and no act of love is greater than sharing God's truth with them.* Much of the backlash came from these lines:

> *Nobody knows what we're for*
> *Only what we're against*
> *When we judge the wounded*
> *What if we put down our signs*

Crossed over the lines
And loved like you did

I received two criticisms. One was from certain pro-life supporters who said, "I can't believe you would suggest that we support abortion."

Oh.

My.

Goodness.

I had to swallow to keep from saying, "Have you heard any of our songs?" How many times do we take the only stance to take, which is pro-life? We flat-out decry abortion in "While You Were Sleeping." In "What If His People Prayed" and "Just Another Birthday," we're clearly pro-life. In fact, we've been more outspoken on the issue than perhaps any other artist. How anyone can see anything else in our songs baffles me.

Here was the rub: The criticism of the lyrics in "Jesus, Friend of Sinners" came from a certain segment of people who think that taking a stand for life means holding signs in the air and yelling at fifteen-year-old girls at their most fragile moment. Does it do any good to scream at girls and women as they walk into a clinic that many of them don't want to walk into anyway?

To these people, I have a few questions: Is that your best effort? Is that your ministry — to scream, "You're killing your child!" at a sixteen-year-old? Remember, she is a child. She doesn't even understand what you're saying because she doesn't hear the word *child* like you hear it. She is one.

Maybe those who are misguided within the pro-life movement could take the six hours they spent planning that day's strategy and the two hours they spent painting signs, spread that eight hours over thirty-minute increments, and meet with teenage girls in their church to disciple them for a period of six or eight weeks. Maybe that would be a more effective way to demonstrate our Creator's love of life.

I think the pro-life movement in many ways needs to make statements, but they're taking up their cause late in the game when they shout at kids outside an abortion clinic. They're several years too late. If we could start by loving on some of these girls who don't have daddies, we could get a lot done.

As a youth pastor, I work with teenagers every day. I work with kids who have broken homes and broken hearts, kids who are being shuffled back and forth between parents and stepparents or even grandparents. Some don't shuffle back and forth at all, because of almost zero parental involvement. Instead, they're raised by their computers and cell phones while the parents work or play.

These kids need mother figures and father figures. To let the media raise them until they start making bad decisions at fourteen or fifteen and then to step back into their lives just in time to yell at them during their lowest moment isn't exactly the best strategy for sound ministry.

Pro-life awareness needs to happen. Education needs to happen. Showing kids when life begins is beautiful, and we all need reminders of these truths. Lobbying Congress and trying to change laws, espousing the sanctity of life, and fighting for the rights of the unborn are essential strategies for followers of Christ. So my problem with the pro-life movement isn't the pro-life movement. My problem is with the screamer method.

One good last-minute alternative is called Save the Storks. This ministry parks its vans outside of abortion clinics to invite girls inside so they can love on them and talk to them about their decision. They try to get to know them and help them work through a variety of options to abortion. Some abortion clinics actually have welcomed Save the Storks to talk to the girls. Love earned Save the Storks the right to speak truth.

The second complaint I got from the song picked on its title. "I love your ministry and I love your music, but I just have a problem with this song because Jesus was not a friend of sinners. Jesus is holy and he can have no fellowship with sin and cannot tolerate sin. We are all enemies of God until we are saved. God cannot have fellowship with sin."

Almost everything in those statements is true. Almost. The word that has gotten lost somewhere in our vocabulary is the word *friend*.

What is a friend? Does a friend approve of everything his friend does? No. When I think of a friend, I ask, "OK, what did Jesus do?" Jesus loved people where they were. He ate lunch with them. He spent time with them. He told them the truth in love. That's all he did, and that's what a friend does.

Nowadays we think that to be a friend with the world

means to sign up and join in with it. But that's not the case. You can be a friend of someone and not agree with the way she lives.

Think about the little kids who ran up to Jesus. He would crouch down and talk to them. He would take them in his lap. He permitted the children to come to him. They were sinners too, yet Jesus loved on them. He ate with tax collectors, the most hated people in society at the time. He touched lepers, the biggest pariahs in town. He treated women with love, dignity, and respect, actions rarely shown by men in those days. That's a friend.

A friend is someone who doesn't judge, because he knows that he will be judged with the same measure of judgment. Jesus called out to Zacchaeus, the sorriest guy in town, and said, "Hey, come down here. I'm going to your house. Let's go eat."

Few people would do that in today's church culture. We would think something like, *Zacchaeus's reputation is known far and wide. If I go to his house, it'll harm my witness.*

When people hurled criticisms of this song, they thought they were giving me a theology lesson on the holiness of God. What I heard through their questions was that they're mad at the world for being lost. Jesus knew that people sinned because they were fallen, steeped in sin, and spiritually empty. "Those who are well have no need of a physician, but those who are sick. I came not to call the righteous, but sinners" (Mark 2:17).

We all see the sinners, and we all judge them.

This woman over here is living a crazy lifestyle and going from guy to guy because she never had a loving dad.

This guy is a constant clown and jerk who shows off and demeans others because no one listens to him at home or work. He needs someone to give him approval, even if it's getting a laugh at someone else's expense.

This guy buys the nicest cars, nicest clothes, and biggest house and never has a hair out of place because he pursues an acceptance he never found at home.

This Goth girl who we all want to write off—she doesn't smile much, but she thinks to herself, *I just fell into this lifestyle, and these people accepted me. Sure, I'll dress in all black. I'll do whatever I have to do. I just want somebody to sit with me at lunch.*

These examples are generalizations that have one thing in common. They're people who long for intimate relationships and acceptance because they've never had it and have never met Jesus. We gravitate to where we are accepted. It's a sad day when the reason so many people remain entrenched in sinful lifestyles is because some of us Jesus people decided, *Jesus wasn't a friend of sinners, and neither am I.*

If all you are is truth, then you're just another blaring sign at an abortion clinic. And that says more about you than it does about the people you target. It says you're ticked off at the world and you don't care whether anyone comes to Jesus.

So I wrote another song for the *Thrive* album. It's called "Love You with the Truth." I wrote it as a sequel to "Jesus, Friend of Sinners." The two songs form an if-then dynamic.

If Jesus is a friend of sinners, then *we* also can love them with the truth.

I hope no one tries to argue the point.

Point to remember

A friend of sinners always finds the balance
between love and truth.

CHAPTER 27

PENDULUM

I've toured the country and much of the world in the last decade. I've met thousands of people of all stripes in many different countries. For decades, these are people who have mostly heard truth without love. "These are the rules. You've broken the rules. You need to start keeping the rules."

In the last few years, I've noticed another tragedy. The pendulum has swung too far the other way. Too many believers are trying to be all love with no truth.

If we stress love so much that we're scared to tell them they need Jesus, we have failed the gospel again. And so a certain megachurch pastor does an interview on national television and effectively says, "I don't want to be the judge of whether Jesus is the only way. I just want to love everybody."

What in the world does that mean? Calling Jesus a liar just to let people know Jesus loves them? Calling himself a pastor of the gospel that clearly points to God's exclusive plan to save people's souls through the death of his Son Jesus and not being willing to say that Jesus himself says he's the only way? That's what happens when we become all love and no truth.

The world doesn't want to hear about rules. Deep down, most people know they're bad and can't stop themselves from doing what they don't want to do. Yet it's equally dangerous to say, "Everybody is going to be OK. Love wins. It's all going to be fine, and everybody gets into heaven." Then why do I need to change anything in my life? The bar is so low that I don't recognize I have an eternal need.

The gospel requires change. The gospel is the good news of a God who makes all things new — which means there are things that need to be made new.

Love earns the right to speak the truth. When you love others, they know you're sharing with them because you love them. Your willingness to share the truth of Scripture proves you really love, and if you're not telling them the truth, you really don't love them. You just love your friendship. Some of us love our friendships more than we love our friends. They're not worth the awkward moment because we don't want to ruin a friendship.

My church showed a video featuring Penn Jillette, an illusionist in the talented duo called Penn and Teller. He talked about a businessman who waited patiently to meet him after a show. The businessman was a stranger from the audience, yet the encounter made a powerful impact on Jillette.

> It was really wonderful. I believe he knew that I was an atheist. But he was not defensive, and he looked me right in the eyes. And he was truly complimentary. It didn't seem like empty flattery. He was really kind and nice and sane and looked me in the eyes and talked to me and then gave me this Bible. And I've always said that I don't respect people who don't proselytize. I don't respect that at all. If you believe that there is a heaven and hell and people could be going to hell or not getting eternal life or whatever, and you think that, well, it's not really worth telling them this because it would make it socially awkward — how much do you have to hate somebody to not proselytize? How much do you have to hate somebody to believe that everlasting life is possible and not tell them that?
>
> I mean, if I believed beyond a shadow of a doubt that a truck was coming at you and you didn't believe it, but that truck was bearing down on you, there is a certain point where I tackle you. And this is more important than that . . .
>
> This guy was a really good guy. He was polite and honest and sane, and he cared enough about me to proselytize and give me a Bible.

In the span of maybe five minutes, this man loved on Jillette with the truth. And it made an indelible impression on an avowed atheist. The only reason we know this story is because Penn Jillette chose to talk about it in a video journal. This proves my final point: When you share your faith with others so they realize you delivered the truth in love and you had no selfish agenda, it lasts.

When we give truth in love, we are ambassadors for Christ. It's not a reflection on us personally. It doesn't matter if the other person rolls her eyes or yells at us or says, "That's cool, but that's not really for me." She still realizes you did it in love, and in quiet moments to come, she will remember it. She's going to lie in bed and look up at the ceiling fan and think about your truth spoken in love.

If someone sends you an anonymous letter, you may read it out of curiosity. But if a *friend* sends you a letter, even if he's dog cussing you, you're going to read every word of it and then reread it. That's your friend. You want to know what your friend says.

A real friend loves his friends despite their sin. A real friend loves them where they are. If you love your friends, sooner or later, you have to tell them the truth. Just do it in love like Jesus did. Because, yes, Jesus was a friend of sinners.

And he still is.

Point to Remember

We fail the gospel when we give love without the truth.

CHAPTER 28

BUILD A BRIDGE

My friend needs help.

My friend has turmoil at home.

My friend's marriage is falling apart.

My friend is on drugs.

My friend is miserable in his job.

My friend's kid is rebelling.

Almost all of us can think of someone who faces at least one of those concerns. If we know of such a problem, if we know that Jesus is the answer, and if we love our friend, how can we respond? Maybe we shouldn't talk first (I tend to speak too soon and try to give all the answers). Maybe a different approach is best.

Let's start with prayer. And then follow up with our friend after we pray.

Do you have a friend who needs Jesus? In your quiet time, take a moment to mention your friend and his problem to God. For me, prayer is like a long text conversation in which I never say good-bye. I always pray with very long pauses.

Anyone who has ever texted me understands this concept. They'll ask me a question and I'll answer, "I think so."

Then they answer back. "Well, what are we going to do?"

Hours later, I finally respond. "OK, how about this?"

That's how I pray too. I never hang up.

"OK, God, here I go. Help me to not blow this conversation."

"All right, God. It seems like something is going on with her today. Please help her and give her wisdom."

I do the same thing for all my friends in need because I believe God can help. It's not like I'm performing some giant missionary work. I just pray for my friend. But guess what I do the next time I hang out with him? I follow up.

"Hey, dude. How's it going with your wife? I've been praying for y'all." That's it. I'm not cracking open Habakkuk on him.

"Hey, bud, I've been praying for you and the kids."

"Yeah, man, it's been crazy."

"I know, I know. I've got your back."

Do you know what I did in that moment? I brought Jesus

into my friendship. There isn't a person reading this book who can't pray for his friend and tell his friend that he's praying for him. Do you know how many of his other friends are praying for him? You're probably the only one, and you've just built a bridge.

Now you have a connection. It takes the relationship to a different depth from the connection you have when you talk about football or career stuff. This is a little more intimate and a lot more meaningful. You don't have all the answers and you don't know all the Greek words of the New Testament, but you have something that lasts an eternity: "I'm praying for you, man."

That builds a bridge to Jesus. Remember, Jesus built a bridge to God for us. We build a bridge to Jesus by loving people and meeting them where they are, praying for them, and sharing truth.

Know Jesus.

Love your friend.

Be a listener.

Pray for your friend.

Follow up.

Build a bridge to Jesus with your words and your life.

You haven't preached a sermon yet. You haven't attended one seminary class. You haven't had to explain creation and evolution.

Here is the last encouragement: pray for a chance to share the gospel if the other person is not a follower of Jesus.

Most of us won't do this. Why? Because we know God will give us a chance, and deep down we're not so sure we really want that. Or even deserve the chance.

We know how wretched we are, and we think we're not worthy to share Jesus. We'd be hypocrites if we tried, we think. But perfect people and perfect answers aren't necessary for the task. True, nobody but Jesus is perfect, but sharing Jesus as flawed believers doesn't mean we're hypocrites. We have to help erase that perception. Nobody knows your scars better than your friends. So own up to them. It takes the pressure off to know that all we have to do is love on people with the truth of who we are and who Jesus is.

A much more challenging obstacle is how to start the conversation when the opportunity comes to share the gospel. Two questions will help broach the subject. Usually, when you get the chance to share your faith, it's because your friend asks you something with a spiritual connotation. But maybe you sense the time is right. Maybe you're sitting in the car or at the pool and you feel God nudging you to pop the question. Here it is: "In your opinion, what does it take for someone to go to heaven?"

This is a great first question that I learned from the FAITH outline while serving as a youth pastor in Daytona Beach. It's an evangelism tool developed by Bobby Welch, my former pastor in Daytona. One of its strengths is that you start by asking the other person's opinion. People like that. Now you have a conversation. We usually don't ask this question because we're afraid our friend is going to answer in a way we didn't anticipate. But there is no plan needed for this question, and you will hear some crazy answers. But most of the time you'll hear common responses: "Well, I don't know. Do good. Don't kill anybody. Do your best." Or, "Oh, I think there are all kinds of different roads that lead there, and everybody has to find their own way."

Are we stumped yet? No. We're just asking a question. But our friend's answer will tell us where she is spiritually.

Second question: "Can I show you how the Bible answers that question?"

Now that may feel uncomfortable. That may feel like you're reading another language. What if the other person answers no? Uh-oh, what do you do? Refer to the first steps.

Know Jesus.

Love your friend.

Keep listening.

Keep praying.

Keep building a bridge with your words and your life.

So you're still good. This is a win.

What if the other person says, "I don't believe the Bible"?

Then try this: "OK, I understand. Let me show you what the Bible says so you can at least know what's in there. Then you can totally rule it out if you don't believe it."

Most people say the Bible is not real only because someone told them that or they saw it on a YouTube video. Sometimes they say it's not real because they want to live like they want and scratch all their itches. It feels better to say there are no rules if you believe there is no ruler. It's easy to say you don't believe in anything.

If at all possible, keep a Bible with you (a Bible app on your cell phone is helpful) and say, "Let me show you a few verses." Have your friend read the verses along with you. It helps to be able to show that what you're saying is in God's Word. So point to it and say, "Here it is right here."

1. *God is holy, and our sin has separated us from him.* That's Romans 3:23.

2. *We're all toast without God, but eternal life through Jesus is God's gift.* That's Romans 6:23.

3. *God loves us and sent Jesus to make us right with him.* Read Romans 5:8.

This is a big verse because most people think, *I need to get better with God.* This verse says that God demonstrated his love for us in that while we were still sinners, Christ died for us. So Jesus built the bridge to God because he knew we weren't good enough. It's too late to get better. We've already sinned. We're not perfect anymore.

4. *Jesus paid the price for our sin.* Flip over to 2 Corinthians 5:20–21.

Our sin cost God. Why can't he just forgive, without repentance or any sort of change on our part? God is holy and just and cannot allow sin into his heaven. It has to be dealt with. In this passage, the word *reconciled* means to be brought back together with God, to be made right with him.

The last verse says God made him who knew no sin to

become sin for us so that we could become the righteousness of God in Christ. You may think that's too confusing. Let's put the pressure on the Word of God. It's strong enough to handle it. Just read the Scripture and tell your friend that God put her sin on Jesus and took Jesus' perfect, sinless righteousness and applied it to her account.

5. *Confess Jesus as Lord and turn away from sin.* Romans 10:9 is gold. It's the verse about confessing with our mouths and believing in our hearts that Jesus is Lord.

The word *repent* usually is associated with large poster boards and crazy people on a street corner. We don't say "repent" a lot these days, but "confess" and "repent" are commands we need to understand. When we truly confess Jesus as *Lord*, we're repenting at that moment.

Becoming a believer requires confessing with your mouth. It means turning your life over to Jesus and saying, "I don't mind anybody knowing this about me." This isn't a quiet prayer in the back of the room. To confess with your mouth that he is Lord—if he is indeed your Lord—means you're willing to do what he says and he's your king. So to repent means to turn away from your sin and to follow Jesus. Just the idea of confessing that he's the Lord of your life is saying, "I'm not in control anymore. I'm going to change."

That is the gospel.

So, what do you say to your friend next? This is what you say: "Is there any reason why you wouldn't want to ask God for forgiveness and give him your life right now?"

Your friend may say yes. She may say no. You may even find yourself in the middle of an awkward moment.

But your friend is worth an awkward moment, isn't she? We're talking about sin, death, and hell. We're talking about forever. You stick out your neck because you love your friend.

What if she says, "I hear what you're saying, but I'm just not ready"? You just have to remember that your friend is not rejecting you personally.

It's OK. No problem. See previous steps.

Know Jesus.

Love your friend.

Keep listening.

Keep praying.

Keep following up.

Keep building a bridge.

What if your friend says she's ready? What if she says, "I can't think of any reason not to do this right here, right now"? Then don't panic. You don't need your pastor on speed dial.

The church tried so hard over the years to train people for this moment that it promoted repeat-after-me prayers. There's not necessarily anything wrong with that, except I'm not sure it allows someone to speak her own heart. I like to hear it come from her. There are no magic words. But it's her heart, and it should be her words.

When I reach this moment with someone, I say, "You can

pray and ask God to forgive you and save you right now. I tell you what, I'll start, and then you say whatever is on your heart."

And then I begin. "God, I'm here with my friend, and she wants to be saved right now. I pray that you will give her tons of peace while she prays."

Then I turn to my friend. "Your turn. Just say what's on your heart."

Some of my friends have blown my mind with the sincerity and realness of their prayers. Others didn't know what to pray. Sometimes I help them through. I just stop and give them a few reminders.

"Hey, just be honest and tell God that you know you're a sinner and that Jesus is his Son, and ask him to forgive you and be your Lord."

She may not be eloquent or get her words in perfect order, but if that is the expression of your friend's heart, she is as saved as the apostle Paul. The key is repentance. Does she have godly sorrow and wish to change? The words of her prayer for salvation are just the outward expression of an inner transformation that only the Holy Spirit can produce.

So only Jesus can save your friend. God did not call you to save your friend. God called you to share the gospel with her. To say you love your friend but then you never share the truth with her means you either don't love your friend or you don't believe the truth.

Your friend may be your spouse or your son or daughter.

Your friend may be one of your parents or a grandparent. Sometimes it's even harder to share with a loved one. But love earns the right to speak truth, and you've earned the right to share what changed your life.

You may share with your friend, only to have her say, "This is awkward. I'm gonna go." If she walks away, you're just going to have to take it. It may be the closest you'll ever come to the book of Acts and having a rock thrown at you. You may get audited by the IRS, but, hey …

What your friend says to you at this moment is not the point. The truth in love is the point. She can laugh in your face. She can fire you. She can shun you at the company picnic or not choose you as her lab partner next semester. But truth is eternal, and she will never forget the truth you shared. Or the love you showed.

Love Jesus.

Show your scars.

Tell your story.

Love 'em with the truth.

That's how you reach out and thrive.

Point to Remember

We build a bridge to Jesus by loving people, praying for them, and sharing truth.

CHAPTER 29

KNEES TO KNEES

Jesus called us to tell people the gospel, but that is only one responsibility. In Matthew 28:19–20, Jesus told his disciples to go do with others what he had done with them. *Go make more of yourselves. Go make disciples.*

In his nature, God is community, and he chooses to include us in the process of creating community. He calls us to a relationship with him and to a relationship with each other. Then he tells us to go out and reach the world.

He says to serve. He says to love. He says to reach out. He even says to love our enemies. None of it is reciprocated. None of it is coming back our way. This is his message: "You've got all the love you need from me. Now get out there and pour into the world. If they steal your coat, give them your undergarment too. If they ask you to go with them a mile, go two. You do whatever you have to do to show them love. By observing the way you love each other, they'll know that I come from God and that you belong to me."

God could have sent some scrolls to twelve guys and told them what to do, but he chose to become a man to befriend and lead them. He actually chose to walk around in dirt with weak people who may or may not believe what he said.

Try to put your head there — to be the God of the universe and have someone say, "I don't know if I'm buying what you're saying."

The humility of Christ described in Philippians 2:3 – 11 is mind-bending. He humbled himself, taking the form of a servant — not just a human being, but a servant human being. We couldn't do that on a micro scale.

Just watch the television show *Undercover Boss* in which a CEO goes undercover to check up on his company. He works in the mail room to see how his company truly functions and how his workers conduct themselves. In some episodes the boss is boiling mad, and you can see him thinking, *You people!* He gets madder as the show moves along.

That would describe us if we walked in Jesus' sandals and saw how others behaved. We wouldn't do so well with unlimited power.

Jesus walked in the flesh and, through patience and parables, boiled down the grandest truths so we could comprehend them. "No, let me explain that again. No, let me explain it again. Nope, not what I said. Let me explain it again. Nope, let me explain it a different way. Good grief. The seed story didn't work. Let's talk about children. Can we talk about kids?"

In humility, he chose to walk around and live life with these twelve guys. He ate with them, traveled with them, laughed with them, and cried with them. Everything was *with them*. Then when he departed, he said, "Now do with others what I just did with you."

I always try to remember the humility of Christ when I go knees to knees with other believers. Notice that it's knees to knees. We all need to be Paul to a few Timothys, one on one in regular talks, walking through Scripture and life together.

If you look back on how you grew as a believer, at every milestone you can usually point back to someone who showed you truth. While we've all had a preacher drop a big bomb of truth and rock our world at some point, it's almost always a parent, a grandmother, a small group leader, a youth pastor, an elder, a deacon, a somebody who taught you something about prayer or about reading the Bible. It wasn't through a sermon. It was through watching how this person lived out what he or she said.

As I grew up, I heard sermons about faith. I heard sermons about trusting God. And then there was Luke Finklestein, the businessman who sat in my eleventh-grade class and talked to us too-cool-for-school teenagers on our level. He told of someone who had not been honest with him and how he chose to take the high road and not be a party to it. He knew one truth: "I'm not just a Christian at church. I'm a Christian at work and everywhere else."

That was huge for me because, when you're a teenager, everyone wants to tell you stuff but not many people take the time to show you anything. The same goes for discipleship.

Young believers need you to do life with them and show them what a Christian looks like in traffic or in the supermarket express line when someone in front of you is buying seventeen items instead of ten. When they see you extend grace and live out what you've shown them in God's Word, it sticks.

The relational model of going to your friend in love and making him a disciple is Christ's idea. Large classes and small groups have their purpose, and I'm a fan. But if you had a hundred people in your church who decided to each disciple one person, it wouldn't just rock your church; it would rock your community.

Usually, though, we wait for someone else to do it.

One of the reasons we don't make disciples is that we think we don't know enough or aren't good enough Christians. We think our friend is going to ask some difficult Bible question that we won't know how to answer. If we're not a Sunday school teacher, we don't think we can do it. We have been conditioned to think that discipleship is buying somebody's workbook and video system and working through a six-week study to fill in all the blanks. Those approaches are worthy and have been key in my own faith. But if that's all you have available and you're not a reader, you're toast.

That's not what discipleship is. It obviously helps to study God's Word together, but most of discipleship is just doing life together and applying Scripture when you get the chance. Discipleship is reproducing yourself. Discipleship is setting an example by doing what you say. Discipleship is just walking with Jesus and taking somebody with you.

Point to Remember

We don't just share the gospel; we also live it with the people God gives us to mentor in the faith.

CHAPTER 30

TWO BOXES

Every believer keeps two boxes lying around. One is a box for God, and the other is a box the believer keeps for himself.

We try to keep God tucked neatly in his box along with everything we think he can do, everything we've ever seen him do, and everything we know about him. For many of us, all we know about him is "forgive me; help me." When anything comes up that's a little outside of what we've seen him do before, we won't let him out of the box to touch it.

We also have a box for ourselves: "These are my talents. This is where people tell me I excel."

Our response to any challenge, opportunity, or question is based on what we keep locked in these two boxes.

I went through the book of Ephesians with my teenage son, John Michael, not long ago. We wound up talking about the question "Why am I here?" I saw the opportunity to use an illustration from his recent experience in helping families interested in adoption.

On a Casting Crowns tour, John Michael worked the booth for Steven Curtis Chapman's Show Hope event for potential adoptive families. At every concert, he trained volunteers on how to hand out information packs and ask the proper questions. It was great for John Michael as he developed his people skills.

"Do you know how big that is?" I asked.

He did what teenage boys do. "Huh?"

Later, we attended the main Show Hope event that attracted people from all over the world. The place was teeming with families with adopted children. Nobody looked like his or her mama, and I didn't know who belonged to whom.

Once we were back home and diving into Ephesians again, I turned to John Michael. "If you think back to that event the other night, you realize adopted kids were all over the place. How many of those packages have you given out at our concerts?"

He looked away and stared as if he were trying to count. "Well, maybe fifty at this concert and forty at that concert and ..." These were all people who had stopped by and picked up a packet as they considered adoption.

"Man, out of fifty potential adoptive families, you know

there is at least one orphan right now who is about to be lifted out of hopelessness and into a family, and it all started with you handing out a packet," I said. "There's a lot more going on than we sometimes realize."

I could see his wheels turn as I tried to give him something concrete to grasp. Then I talked about his BroSis partner. Bro-Sis is one of our youth ministries. We match younger kids with more mature ones who encourage them and answer questions. John Michael hadn't considered his impact on his little partner. I reminded him how huge it is when you're small to have an older kid hang out with you and tell you you're doing well and you're wearing a cool shirt. It changes your whole day.

"A lot of times, we keep God in this little box of what we think he can do," I said. "So when we encounter a problem that we've never seen him handle or that a specific Scripture doesn't address, we think, *God really can't help me with this problem with my friend.* But you've seen in our recent studies on friendships that God really does care about friendships."

"Yeah," he said.

"We got out of the box and saw that God is bigger than you thought. Well, he's bigger than you think in a lot of ways. He's bigger than things you might be struggling with, things you think about at night that you know you're not supposed to be thinking about but your mind is racing and you're trying to go to sleep and you can't."

I talked about his thought life because boys always make themselves the hero in some fantasy land. They're Superman, and everyone needs them.

"God is big enough to help you with that stuff. But, guess what, it's the same thing with you. We all put ourselves in a box too. We think, *That guy is good at that, and this guy is good at this. I'm not really great at anything. I'll just let them be the leader, and I'll be the clown,*" I said. "We decide for ourselves what God can do and what we can do. You've heard my story your whole life. In high school, I wasn't good at anything I'm doing right now. I graduated with none of this in my head."

John Michael nodded because he's heard my story countless times. When I graduated from high school, I didn't think about one thing I'm doing now. All I thought was, *Draw pictures.* Somehow, I wanted to make a living as an artist because I could sketch pretty pictures. But I had myself in this little box, and I had God in a box. But the more I get into his Word and the more I talk with him and see him answer my prayers, the more I build my spiritual vocabulary. My spiritual context grows. I start seeing with his eyes. I see more about God; I see more about myself; and I see that he wants us to rip open the boxes.

We are not alone in our struggle with a lack of faith. In Matthew 17, Jesus rebukes his disciples for their little faith. "If you have faith like a grain of mustard seed, you will say to this mountain, 'Move from here to there,' and it will move, and nothing will be impossible for you" (verse 20).

When you first dive into the Word and grow the roots of your faith, like newborn babes you crave spiritual milk. Later, Paul effectively says, "I'm giving you guys milk because that's where you are, but now you need to get into the meat and start growing even deeper" (Hebrews 5:12).

This is why I have stressed our need to learn who God is and who we are.

I read James when I was twenty-one, and I read James a week ago. I looked at some verses and thought, *There's no way that verse was in there when I was twenty-one. How in the world did I miss something like that?* As you grow closer to God, you build his vocabulary in your heart. You learn how he moves and speaks, and you grasp more from him than just "stop doing bad things and start doing good things." You see his providence.

I didn't know how to pray for a marriage when I was a young believer. I didn't know how to counsel a pregnant teenager. I didn't know how to talk to someone struggling with homosexuality. I didn't have a file for any of that. You'll notice that none of those examples involve singing songs. The closer you grow to God, the more he knocks out the walls and takes you somewhere new.

As I grow my roots, I constantly learn. There's no finish line, not until we reach heaven. As long as I'm wearing skin, I have to dig into the Word. Grasping who God is and who I am in Christ will affect how I reach out to others.

But we get scared, don't we? God has so much more for us than our spiritual paralysis. Remember Philippians 2:12, where God tells us to work out what he has worked into us? This is the primary area where fear and a lack of faith thwart what God wants to do with us.

We pray for the Lord to use us, and he answers with opportunities to serve him. The thing is, most of our plans are more self-aggrandizing than God's plans for us. He wants us to serve him where he planted us. The part of your life that you consider humdrum is exactly where Jesus wants to reach people through you.

You're sitting at Thanksgiving dinner and you've been praying for your family for a month, and out of nowhere Uncle Joe looks at you and says, "So, what's all this Bible stuff y'all believe?"

Adrenaline shoots straight to your heart, and you think, *This is my shot. This is what I've been praying for.* And you choke. I don't see how you can be a believer and not have experienced something like this at least once. Failure is a part of the process, but God will bring us back to the same point until we get it. Until we obey.

"All right, you've been digging in and trusting me," he says. "Now let me redefine some things for you because it's time to jump."

These are our chances to thrive. This is what the Thrive life is all about.

"All right, you've prayed for your friend. Let's do it. Talk to him."

"OK, you've wanted to give, and you've been praying about it. You've been in the Word, and you read that book on biblical stewardship. Well, this family needs gas money."

Again and again, a persistent God taps on our shoulder.

"Hey, you've been asking for opportunities to share and lead,

*and your pastor for small groups just asked for volunteers to lead
a class. It's time."*

It's as if God smiles at us and tells us to shut up and jump.

Panama City, Florida, is a tourist trap with sugar-sand
beaches. It has a long strip with places to rent scooters, ride
go-carts, and bungee jump. You can pay $20 for a stranger
named Skip to tie a rubber band around your waist so you
can jump from a nosebleed-high platform. It makes perfect
sense when you're on the ground. You just know it's going to
be awesome. You gaze up and it looks high but not all that
high, so you walk up the stairs. You're probably a good two
or three flights up before you look down for the first time.
That's when you realize your heart is pounding through your
temples.

Then you reach the top and meet Skip right before you
look over the side. Skip has to pry your white knuckles off
the rail so he can fasten the strap around you. Skip is maybe
seventeen. He's running the show, and hopefully he paid
attention when he tied all of those knots eight hours ago.
You're pretty sure he's been wearing those clothes for about
four days.

Normally, Skip and you wouldn't hang out much. You
probably wouldn't invite him to dinner. But suddenly you
feel the need to talk for a while. Let's just hang out. "How
long have you been doing this, Skip? Tell me about yourself."

Skip grins as he stands in front of the gate that opens to

the jump platform. Skip moves out of the way, and you see why he is smiling. On the gate is a sign with bold letters: SHUT UP AND JUMP. Skip will tell you the sign is there for a reason. When people finally reach the jumping point, they want to talk. The longer they stand there and talk, the less likely they are to jump.

One of Skip's jobs is to get them to shut up quickly, and he starts counting. "Ready? One, two ..."

"Hold on, hold on. *I'll* count. Let me count before I jump."

But the ones who ask to count never count. If they step up to that line two or three times, it's not going to happen.

Skip's sign reminds me of what happens in our walk with the Lord. We know exactly what he wants. He tells us it's time to get serious about digging into roots and seeking him with our whole hearts. It's time to establish a regular prayer time. It's time to commit to knowing God and making him known. It's time to reach out and go on a mission trip or visit a nursing home. It's time to share the gospel with a coworker.

We, meanwhile, want to start counting. "Well, maybe we can do one more workbook. Let me listen to this new podcast I got today. Maybe I should do a little more training." We're trained well beyond our obedience.

Jesus sees our hesitance, grins like Skip as he reminds us of our eternal tether to him, and points to the sign. "You asked for this. Here's your chance," he says. "Your weakness doesn't bother me. Your past doesn't bother me. I don't need you. I *want* you. Let's go."

It seems like he's said it to me a thousand times. So with a smile on my face and all of the love of Jesus in my heart, I now say it to you: What's holding you back? What are you waiting for?

Shut up and jump.

Point to Remember

We box in God and ourselves with wrong perceptions;
God says jump.

CONCLUSION

The enormous tree at The Junction in Alabama thrives because it is living and breathing and growing on its own root system.

Yet that giant oak tree features something else. Moss hangs from its branches. The moss is not like the tree. The only way the moss survives is to live off something else. We have to remind ourselves every day — several times a day — that we weren't meant to survive. We're meant to thrive.

Say it with me: *I was never meant to survive. I was meant to thrive.*

The reason a lot of us are merely surviving is that we're living off other people. Even as believers, what keeps us going is somebody else's excitement, somebody else's sermon, somebody else's song, somebody else's success, somebody else's ministry. As long as we're with them, it's awesome. But that's not thriving. That's being moss.

Fellowship is great, but fellowship is not our foundation. We have to build on Jesus. He's the foundation.

The Walking Dead on AMC has been one of the most popular shows on TV for the last few years. It's about zombies, and it's filmed about an hour from where I live. When you look at a zombie, that's what surviving looks like. That's what religion looks like. The zombie can walk. It moves around and makes noises. It eats. I won't say what it eats, but it eats. Still, nothing is happening on the inside. It's lifeless. My fear is that the world has formed a picture of religion and has tied the church to that picture. My fear is that they view the church as a bunch of dead zombies.

In Matthew 23, Jesus rails against the Pharisees for being the walking dead: "Woe to you, scribes and Pharisees, hypocrites! For you are like whitewashed tombs, which outwardly appear beautiful, but within are full of dead people's bones and all uncleanness. So you also outwardly appear righteous to others, but within you are full of hypocrisy and lawlessness" (verses 27 – 28).

Those who thrive have an abundant life. Those who survive almost always fall into religion.

If you've ever seen me in concert or on a video, I'm sure you haven't noticed this, but I have what they call a little bit of a weight problem. I know, I know, it's slight — almost imperceptible. Go on YouTube and check out a Casting Crowns video, and you'll have to strain to see it on the close-ups. A lot of people have asked me, "Why do you always wear black T-shirts?" Black is slimming. You should see me in orange. I look like the Great Pumpkin in Charlie Brown.

I decided I was going to do something about my weight, but I don't have a lot of discipline. So I had to burn my bridges and make wholesale, drastic changes. I decided that for a full calendar year I would drink no soft drinks and no sweet tea. If you're from up North or the West Coast, I'm not sure you're into the beauty of sweet tea. It's pretty much pancake syrup on ice, and down South we regard it as nectar from heaven. I made up my mind to forgo it for the first time in my life and drink only water and juices.

I got fired up. I went on Twitter and zinged it to my followers. I called it the HydroForce plan, and people actually joined me in the yearlong endeavor.

Several weeks into it, I had a sudden attack of allergies. I think my immune system recoiled. The first thing the nurse made me do was step on the scales. I hadn't touched a soft drink or sweet tea for months. And the scales said I was fatter than ever.

I had one thought. *I'm walking out of this room. I'm going to Wendy's. I'm going to get a vat of Coke and a vat of sweet tea, and I'm going to hook them up in an IV tube to my arm for a week.*

I was so angry.

Look at all of this stuff I'm not doing. Why am I not smaller?

I went home and told Melanie. She raised her eyebrows

and cocked her head. "Well, you could exercise a little," she said.

I didn't want to hear that. So I did what I always do. I looked for a way to turn it into a sermon illustration.

The truth that hit me was that sometimes we think we're going to get somewhere just by *not* doing stuff, by cutting things out of our lives. Sometimes we think we're Christians because of the things we don't do and where we don't go. We think, *I love Jesus, so I'm not going to do any of this stuff.* We cut it off, which is a good thing, but we don't add anything to ourselves. It's like a diet without exercise.

It's great that I guard my new life from certain influences and tastes that I acquired in my old life. But if that's all I'm doing, then it's just a big behavior diet. I also must plant into my new life. I encourage you to do more than refuse to do certain things. I encourage you to dig deep into Scripture and to discipline yourself in prayer. When you read a verse, ask questions. "Lord, what are you showing me about you? What are you showing me about me? Is there anything you're asking me to take out of my life? Is there anything you're asking me to put into my life? Are you making me a promise in this verse? What characters in the story I just read do I most resemble, and what can I learn from them? What do you want to teach me?"

When we add to our lives the wonder and power of Scripture, prayer, and obedience, we leave surviving in the dust and discover how to thrive.

I remember when I first learned this truth. I had never

really pursued a "quiet time" to take my relationship with Jesus to a personal level. I turned to the book of James as a young man because it was only five chapters long. I figured even I could handle five chapters.

That study through James put me on a path of personal devotion that I maintain to this day. Have I been perfect? No. But I've been faithful. I've chased after God's heart, and I learned that when a believer chases after God's heart, God makes sure the believer catches it.

God isn't a mystical figure in the heavens who plays a mischievous game of hide-and-seek. He is a personal God who invades your life through the person of the Holy Spirit and longs for you to "feed" the life of Christ in you with his Word and with prayer and then allow the results to reach out into other people's lives.

If we sow to the flesh and pursue life on our own terms, we will from the flesh reap corruption. But if we sow to the Spirit, we will from the Spirit reap eternal life (Galatians 6:8). So if we don't develop the spiritual disciplines of Bible study and prayer, we live more off of our own instincts than his Word and will never hear his voice enough to know where he wants us to serve him. Any efforts we make on our own will be empty and powerless.

When you truly surrender your will to his, seek his heart, hear his voice, and respond to his nudges, you thrive. It doesn't take long to realize that life is radically different and you're no longer just surviving. Suddenly, life resonates with a deep-seated—almost inexplicable—joy and peace that flow from a Father who is well pleased.

I've said nothing about money, stature, prestige, or success. Instead, I've talked about giving up your rights, laying down your claim to yourself, and letting Jesus have all of you.

When I finally let go and started pursuing an intimacy with Jesus, when I finally stopped dictating how I would live my life, he orchestrated a stunning path for me. Never in my wildest dreams would I have conceived of writing and singing hit songs that play on the radio, selling millions of records, selling out arenas, winning a Grammy, or singing in Communist North Korea and for the president of the United States. I didn't even conceive of standing before a roomful of teenagers and teaching them about the Lord.

But when I said yes to Jesus—and really let my yes be yes—he smiled big. And he said, "Now let me show you what I have for you."

I don't promise that God will give you a hit record or put you on stage in front of thousands of people. I don't promise that he will heal every disease in this life and pay every bill. But I do know that when you let Jesus have all of you, he will fulfill his purpose for your life and show you exactly why he created you for himself. I also know you will experience a contentment right where you are and in whatever he has for you. This contentment comes from an assurance that God is right there with you and that he'll never leave you. And it comes from knowing you are his and that your life shows you love Jesus.

It all started for me when I finally yielded to Jesus and cracked open the book of James for earnest study. I made it a habit to feed my roots with God's Word. I learned how to talk to God. I learned how to listen to him. Then, over time I learned how to follow his still small voice. The result has been a life more abundant than I ever could have imagined.

Now my life verses are the Thrive Verses. I sign "Psalm 1" on every autograph I write. But it's more than just a post-script to a fan. It also reminds *me* that a man who delights in God's Word is like a tree planted by streams of living water. He yields fruit and prospers.

The prophet Jeremiah offered a parallel to Psalm 1. He wrote that the man who trusts in man (including trusting in oneself) and makes flesh his strength is cursed. He's like a shrub in the desert that won't see any good come. But then he offers this one option in Jeremiah 17:7 – 8:

> Blessed is the man who trusts in the LORD,
>   whose trust is the LORD.
> He is like a tree planted by water,
>   that sends out its roots by the stream,
> and does not fear when heat comes,
>   for its leaves remain green,
> and is not anxious in the year of drought,
>   for it does not cease to bear fruit.

May you trust in Jesus and send out your roots by the stream of his living water. May you endure the wilting heat of fear and life's anxieties. May you dig deep to know God, reach out to make him known, and thrive all the rest of your days.

THE THRIVE CHALLENGE

DIGGING IN

I will dig in to my root system by seeking to strengthen my relationship with God.

This means growing in your faith. This means going to church and diving in to worship time. Take your Bible. Take notes. Stay engaged. Review the notes and Scripture references afterward. Pray all week about the points you learned. Pore over Scripture every day, including weekends, and ask God to speak to you through his Word and his Holy Spirit.

I will get involved in a small group.

Community is key. You don't need to be an attender. You need to be an engager, a builder. You need to become an integral part of the class and, therefore, a kingdom builder. If you attend worship and nothing else, your only fellowship is to wait for someone to talk to you during greeting time. You won't grow as much as you would in the safety of those like yourself. You have to be in a small group of like-minded believers who realize they can't do life alone.

REACHING OUT

I will find a regular service opportunity I'm passionate about and do it.

The only way to be the hands and feet of Jesus is to obey him and serve others. If our Creator God can wash the sweaty, filthy feet of men who wore sandals, we can humble ourselves and put others ahead of ourselves.

I will commit to share Jesus with people I know who need him.

Think about what Penn Jillette said (chapter 27). How much do we have to hate someone to know the only way that leads to eternal life and not share it with that person? Know Jesus. Love your friend. Be a listener. Pray for your friend. Follow up.

I will go on a mission.

When you plug into a small group, more than likely at some point you'll have an opportunity to work on a short-term mission project either locally or abroad. Even if your small group doesn't pursue a mission emphasis, you can seek one through your church.

I will live on purpose.

Your purpose is to know God and make him known. Your purpose is to point to the one true God, Jesus Christ. All believers should commit to being purposeful in their relationships and in living out the gospel. Share your story. Show your scars. Tell people about Jesus and the hope found only in him. Always be ready to give the reason for that hope (1 Peter 3:15).

DIGGING IN AND REACHING OUT
In both digging in and reaching out, I will ask God to help me thrive.

In your own words, ask God every day to make you look more like Jesus and less like yourself. Your prayer might sound something like this:

God, I'm going to dive into this ministry and into daily time in your Word. I want to pour into the root system of my faith. Instead of just trying to be better, I ask you to grow me into a thriving believer. I don't want to survive this year. I want to thrive.

To take the Thrive Challenge to a deeper level, go to www.castingcrowns.com.

ACKNOWLEDGMENTS

Any book is a monumental undertaking, but when you're trying to make an album at the same time, it can be especially challenging. Without the talent and hard work of some godly folks, I wouldn't have been able to get all of this out of my head and into a book.

Tim Luke has been my friend and coworker for twelve years. We've written four books together, and he has learned my heart and my teaching voice. I'm grateful for his talent but mostly for his friendship. Thanks, bro.

As always, my literary agent, Steve Green, was a great steward of the process. Thank you for your guidance and help.

I appreciate the expertise and wisdom of editor Carolyn McCready and her gifted team at Zondervan. Thank you for improving this book and helping us send out a passionate message.

Finally, thank you to my church family at Eagle's Landing First Baptist Church. You have always supported and encouraged me, and I'm blessed to be able to call all of you friends. My prayer is that we keep loving one another.

Thrive Student Edition

Digging Deep, Reaching Out

*Mark Hall Pastor and Lead
Singer of Casting Crowns
with Tim Luke*

You've probably heard the words "live out your faith" dozens, if not hundreds, of times, but what does that phrase really mean? And how do you really follow Jesus in today's world?

In this student adaptation of his book, *Thrive*, Casting Crowns' Mark Hall explores exactly what it means when your faith and your life collide, and how you can take the next steps in making that faith real and evident to those around you. Using relatable stories and applications you can use, as well as sharing some life lessons, Hall show how you can root yourself in the truth and grow strong in your beliefs as you become the person God designed you to be.

Available in stores and online!

Your Own Jesus

A God Insistent on Making It Personal

*Casting Crowns' Mark Hall
with Tim Luke*

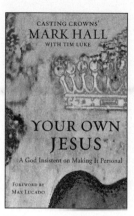

Casting Crowns' lead singer Mark Hall asks, "Do you have your own Jesus?"

Why do you feel close to God one minute and so far away the next? Why does your faith seem empty? Why is it so easy to compromise with the world?

Perhaps it's because we have merely inherited someone else's Jesus, relying on what we've seen and heard from family, friends, or pastors.

A true storyteller and a teacher with a heart for ministry, Mark Hall traces the downward spiral caused by spiritual compromise with the world, and then charts the upward road to wholeness and health that comes when we claim our very own Jesus.

You need to discover your own Jesus. The real Jesus. The one who wants you to be honest, committed, and uncompromising. The one who is waiting to have a relationship with you.

Move past imitating a religion to experiencing a relationship that is vibrant, personal, and fulfilling.

The Well

Why Are So Many Still Thirsty?

Mark Hall with Tim Luke

A compelling and inspiring dip into the one true well.

Using the powerful story of the woman at the well found in the gospel of John, *The Well* takes a passionate look at the real reason that even the most charmed of lives are empty when they lack the one element that makes us whole.

Grammy Award-winning singer and songwriter Mark Hall illustrates from his own life how the "dry holes" of accomplishments, possessions, relationships, and many of the other goals we work toward can never fully satisfy us. Their rewards are temporary and often divert us from God's offer of abundant, refreshing, sustaining life. *The Well* leads us to the life-changing conclusion that we can never be truly satisfied until we go to Jesus and receive from him the living water that will never run dry and will quench our thirst forever.